Divine Echoes: Poems of Prophets, Faith, & Redemption

Leah Niffhondro

Published by Leah Niffhondro, 2024.

DIVINE ECHOES: POEMS OF PROPHETS, FAITH, & REDEMPTION

First edition. August 19, 2024.

ISBN: 979-8227237927

Written by Leah Niffhondro.

Table of Contents

In the Beginning

In the void, where silence reigned,
Where darkness veiled all that could be,
There whispered a Voice, ancient and unchained,
"Let there be light," and light broke free.
From the breath of that Voice, life was sown,
The waters danced, the heavens were stirred,
And from the deep, a world unknown,
Took shape with the power of a single word.
The sky was painted in hues of dawn,
The earth, a canvas of endless might,
Mountains rose, and rivers were drawn,
As day was born from the womb of night.
Stars were cast like jewels on black,
The moon was hung to rule the tide,
And in the sun's warm, golden track,
Time began its endless stride.
The land gave birth to the seeds of life,
Each blade of grass, each towering tree,
And in the wind's sweet, gentle strife,
The breath of God set creation free.
In oceans vast and skies of blue,
The creatures swam, the birds took flight,
And in their song, a promise true,

That life would flourish, pure and bright.
Then came the crown of all He made,
In His own image, He formed from clay,
A heart that beat, a soul that prayed,
Man and woman, to walk His way.
He breathed in them a spark divine,
Gave them dominion, a sacred trust,
To tend the earth, both yours and mine,
From dawn till dusk, from dust to dust.
He saw the world, and it was good,
A tapestry of love and grace,
And in the stillness, there He stood,
A smile upon His holy face.
On the seventh day, He ceased His hand,
And rested in the work He'd done,
The heavens and earth, both sea and land,
In harmony with the rising sun.
In the beginning, there was light,
And from the light, a world was born,
A song of love, a dream of might,
Etched in the stars of every dawn.
For in each dawn, the story lives,
Of how the world began to spin,
A tale of hope, a gift that gives,
A glimpse of God's eternal hymn.

The Fall

In Eden's heart, where peace once lay,
Amidst the trees, the rivers' play,
A serpent whispered, smooth as night,
And darkness stirred in Eden's light.
A garden blessed, where life began,
Where God had walked with woman, man,
The air was sweet, the skies were clear,
And every creature knew no fear.
But in the midst, a single tree,
Held fruit of knowledge, wild and free,
Of good and evil, truth and lies,
A test beneath those tranquil skies.
The serpent coiled with cunning grace,
A smile upon its twisted face,
"Did God say you must not partake?
This fruit won't kill, but you'll awake."
Eve paused, her gaze upon the prize,
The fruit that held the world's disguise,
And in its shine, she saw a lure,
A promise of a truth unsure.
"Eat," it hissed, "and you will see,
Your eyes will open, you'll be free,
Like God, you'll know both right and wrong,

3

LEAH NIFFHONDRO

This knowledge will make you strong."
Her hand reached out, the choice was made,
The line was crossed, the price was paid,
She took and ate, and with a breath,
She ushered in the shadow of death.
To Adam, then, she passed the fruit,
A gesture that would take their root,
From soil of life to ground of pain,
As innocence began to wane.
And with that bite, the veil was torn,
The world they knew, now stained, forlorn,
Their eyes were opened, shame unveiled,
Their purity now lost, assailed.
They saw their nakedness, their sin,
And fear and guilt crept deep within,
They hid from God, who called their name,
But nothing now could be the same.
"Who told you that you were unclothed?
Have you eaten from the tree I loathed?"
The voice of God, both sad and stern,
Spoke of the path they could not return.
The serpent cursed to crawl in dust,
A life of toil, a broken trust,
For Eve, the pangs of birth and life,
For Adam, sweat, and endless strife.
Banished from Eden's perfect grace,
They wandered out, their rightful place,
Guarded now by flaming sword,
A world once blessed, now scarred and flawed.
The echo of that fateful choice,

Still rings within our human voice,
For in their fall, we find our own,
In every heart, the seed is sown.
But even in the shadow's grip,
A promise lingered on their lips,
That one would come to crush the head,
Of evil's serpent, death, and dread.
So in the fall, a hope was born,
A glimmer in the darkest morn,
For though we walk in sin's cruel thrall,
God's love still reaches, after all.
In every tear, in every pain,
We feel the weight of Eden's stain,
But also hear, a distant call,
A whisper of redemption's thrall.
For even as we bear the cost,
Of Eden's innocence now lost,
The promise lives, the Word remains,
That we might rise from sin's dark chains.
And so the story, fierce and bold,
Of Adam, Eve, the serpent cold,
Reminds the world of love's great fall,
And yet, the hope that saves us all.

Whispers of Rain

In the quiet before the storm, the earth sighed,
A world awash in shadows, where the light had died.
Men walked with giants, hearts heavy with sin,
A place where darkness festered deep within.
The Lord looked down, His heart filled with grief,
For the world He had crafted had turned like a leaf.
Violence echoed in the valleys and the hills,
And the cry of the earth rose, against man's ill wills.
Yet in the midst of the chaos, a man walked alone,
Noah, the righteous, whose heart was God's own.
He found grace in the eyes of the One who sees all,
A beacon of hope in a world doomed to fall.
"Build an ark," came the whisper, the command from above,
"For a flood shall come, not of hatred but love."
To cleanse and to purify, to start anew,
The earth shall be washed by the skies' weeping dew.
With hands weathered by time, he built with care,
An ark for the creatures, two of each pair.
The hammer's rhythm, a heartbeat of hope,
As the heavens gathered, darkened with scope.
The animals came, led by a force unseen,
From the fierce lion to the ant, small and keen.
And Noah, with his family, entered the wooden womb,

DIVINE ECHOES: POEMS OF PROPHETS, FAITH, & REDEMPTION

While the earth outside trembled, awaiting its doom.
The skies broke open, a torrent unleashed,
As the fountains of the deep surged, never to cease.
For forty days and nights, the waters did rise,
And the earth was submerged beneath the weeping skies.
But in that floating cradle, through the storm's fierce call,
Was a promise kept, that life would not fall.
And when the waters receded, the ark found its rest,
On the peaks of Ararat, where the dove built its nest.
Noah stepped forth, on the cleansed, reborn ground,
And there in the heavens, a rainbow was found.
A covenant of colors, a vow to uphold,
That never again would the waters enfold.
So remember the flood, and the ark, and the rain,
A story of judgment, of loss, and of gain.
For in the waters that swept the old world away,
Was the seed of tomorrow, and a brand new day.

The Tower of Babel: A Poem of Ambition and Ruin

In the dawn of a world, fresh from the flood's purge,
Man walked with pride, no longer on the verge.
One language, one voice, a people as one,
They sought to reach the heavens, to challenge the sun.
"Come, let us build," said the hearts filled with fire,
"A tower to the sky, to mark our desire.
Let us make a name, lest we be scattered,
Across the earth, where we once were shattered."
Brick by brick, they raised their spire,
Fueled by ambition, their souls full of fire.
The tower climbed, defying the skies,
As man, in his pride, sought to rise.
But in the heavens, the Creator watched,
As His children forgot the lessons He'd taught.
Their unity, now twisted with pride,
Threatened to topple, to cast them aside.
"Let Us go down," said the voice of the Lord,
"And see what they build, what dreams they hoard.
For if as one they dare reach so high,
What then will stop them from claiming the sky?"
With a breath from the heavens, the tongues were confused,
A babble of voices, where words were misused.

No longer could they speak, no longer could they share,
The dreams they once held, dissolved in the air.
The tower stood silent, its builders dispersed,
Across the earth, with languages cursed.
No longer as one, they scattered like sand,
The dream of Babel, a ruin in the land.
And so it remains, a lesson of old,
Of pride and ambition, and the stories we're told.
For man may rise, but fall he will,
When he forgets the power of a greater will.
The Tower of Babel, a monument tall,
To the hubris of man, and the great fall.
A warning etched in the winds that blow,
That we are but stewards of the seeds we sow.

The Call of Abram: A Wild Odyssey

In the land of Ur, where idols reign,
Amidst the dust and the clamor, the profane,
A voice broke through, not soft, but fierce,
A thunderous whisper, the heavens pierced.
"Abram!" it called, with a fire unquenched,
"Leave your father's house, from all you're entrenched.
Forsake the familiar, the gods of stone,
To a land unknown, where you'll walk alone."
No map was given, no stars aligned,
Just a voice, wild as the desert wind.
"Go!" it thundered, "Go without delay,
For in your seed, a nation will sway."
But oh, the madness, the sheer, wild leap,
To abandon all for a promise to keep.
Sarai by his side, her laughter a knife,
As they journeyed into the unknown, leaving behind life.
The Canaanite lands, with their strange gods and kings,
Felt the footsteps of a man with unearthly wings.
But famine struck, cruel and unkind,
Pushed to Egypt, Abram's faith entwined.
"Say you're my sister," he told his bride,
To Pharaoh's courts, where truth would hide.
But the lies birthed plagues, a curse unforeseen,

As Abram's God stirred in the unseen.
Pharaoh cast him out, with riches untold,
A twist in the tale, a fortune of gold.
Back to Canaan, the promise still raw,
A man with the world at his feet, yet in awe.
"Look to the stars," the voice roared again,
"Count them if you can, beyond the ken.
So shall your offspring be, countless and free,
A nation born from your faith in Me."
But where is the heir, the seed of this vow?
The years pass by, no child to endow.
Yet Abram stood firm, wild-eyed, crazed,
Believing in promises through the haze.
Then came the day, the covenant was sealed,
A ceremony strange, with blood revealed.
A flaming torch passed through the night,
Abram stood stunned, in the flickering light.
From the madness of Ur to the altars of stone,
Abram wandered, yet never alone.
His journey a riddle, wild and profound,
A promise in chaos, where faith is found.
So let the world shake, let reason defy,
For in the wild, where the impossible lies,
Is the call of Abram, a journey untamed,
Where destiny's forged and faith is named.

The Covenant of Stars

In the hush of the night, beneath a velvet sky,
Abram stood, weary, with questions piled high.
The years had passed, promises yet unfulfilled,
A heart burdened, but a spirit still thrilled.
"Fear not, Abram," the voice echoed deep,
"I am your shield, your reward you'll keep."
But Abram sighed, his voice cracked with pain,
"Lord, what will You give, for childless I remain."
"My heir is a stranger, no seed of my own,
The promise You made seems buried, overthrown."
But the Lord, with a whisper, a fire in His breath,
Called Abram out, to the edge of the earth.
"Look to the heavens, count if you dare,
The stars that dance in the midnight air.
So shall your offspring be, countless as these,
A nation born from faith, on a wandering breeze."
Abram gazed up, his doubts washed away,
By the tapestry of stars in their vast array.
In that moment, his heart swelled with trust,
In the God who breathed life into the dust.
"Know this, Abram, your journey's not done,
Your descendants shall rise with the morning sun.
But first, they'll wander in lands not their own,

For four hundred years, in a world overthrown."
"But I will judge the nation they serve," said the Lord,
"And they shall come out with riches untold.
To this land, your descendants will return,
And here they'll build, as the world will turn."
A darkness fell, deep as the grave,
And Abram saw visions, wild and brave.
A smoking firepot, a blazing torch,
Passed between the pieces, under heaven's porch.
On that day, the Lord made a vow,
A covenant sealed in blood, here and now.
"To your offspring, I give this land,
From the Nile to the Euphrates' strand."
Abram believed, and it was counted as right,
A faith as old as the first dawn's light.
For in that moment, beneath the starry sea,
God and man walked in a mystery.
The promise of nations, the birth of a dream,
In the silence of night, where the stars gleam.
A covenant eternal, unbroken, untamed,
In the heart of Abram, where God's fire is framed.

14

The Laughter of Isaac: A Poem of Unbelievable Joy

In the twilight of years, where hope fades to dust,
Where the body grows weary, and dreams turn to rust,
There lived an old man, his name whispered with awe,
Abram, now Abraham, by the promise of law.
Beside him, his bride, her laughter once dry,
Sarai, now Sarah, with a glint in her eye.
For years they had wandered, with a promise untamed,
A child to be born, and a nation unnamed.
But who could believe, in the womb so barren,
In the belly of time, where silence had been?
A laugh escaped her, bitter and wild,
At the thought of her wrinkled form bearing a child.
Yet the Lord's voice broke through, soft as the dawn,
"Is anything too hard for the One who's withdrawn?
By this time next year, your joy will arrive,
In the form of a son, a miracle alive."
And so it was written, in the stars above,
A testament of grace, and of God's boundless love.
The earth held its breath, the heavens leaned near,
As the promise took shape, in the quiet, no fear.
The months rolled by, a mystery profound,
As Sarah's laughter turned, a new joy found.

Her belly swelled with the impossible dream,
A prophecy fulfilled, like a river's stream.
Then came the day, the world stood still,
As the tent filled with cries, a thrill, a chill.
Sarah held in her arms the child of her mirth,
A boy named Isaac, the laughter of earth.
She laughed again, but now it was pure,
The sound of a promise, a joy so sure.
"Who would have said," she cried with delight,
"That Sarah would nurse, in the dim of the night?"
But this was no ordinary child, no common birth,
He was the seed of nations, the hope of the earth.
Through Isaac, the world would come to know,
The power of a God who makes barren things grow.
The angels sang, the stars danced wild,
For unto them was born a covenant child.
The laughter of Sarah echoed through time,
A song of faith, a rhythm, a rhyme.
For in that child, all things were revealed,
The beginning of a story, a destiny sealed.
Isaac, the laughter, the miracle given,
A shock to the world, a glimpse into heaven.
And so they rejoiced, in the twilight years,
With a joy so profound, it washed away fears.
For Isaac was born, against all the odds,
A testament to the faithfulness of God.

The Binding of Isaac: A Wild and Shocking Test

In the stillness of dawn, where shadows retreat,
A voice called out, sharp, impossible, sweet.
"Abraham!" it thundered, tearing the sky,
"Take your son, your only son, and let him die."
Isaac, the laughter, the promised seed,
Now became the vessel of a terrifying deed.
"To the land of Moriah, where altars burn,
Offer him there, and do not return."
Abraham's heart, a storm in his chest,
Yet faith held him firm, refusing to rest.
He saddled the donkey, took wood and the knife,
And with Isaac beside him, walked the edge of life.
Three days they journeyed, the silence thick,
Each step a betrayal, each breath a prick.
Isaac, with innocence, questioned the fire,
"Father, where is the lamb for this pyre?"
Abraham trembled, his voice barely clear,
"God will provide, my son, do not fear."
But within him a battle, wild and fierce,
As faith and love clashed, each seeking to pierce.
They reached the place, a hill of dread,
Where the earth seemed to shudder beneath their tread.

LEAH NIFFHONDRO

With hands that betrayed not the storm inside,
Abraham bound Isaac, his tears unsupplied.
The boy, with trust, lay silent and still,
As his father raised the knife, bending to will.
But oh, the agony, the silent scream,
Of a father torn in a nightmarish dream.
The blade hovered high, the heavens held breath,
A moment suspended between life and death.
And then—! A voice, a cry from the sky,
"Abraham! Abraham! Do not let him die!"
A ram in the thicket, caught by its horns,
A substitute, a salvation, as the covenant mourns.
Abraham fell, trembling, wild with relief,
As the promise of God cut through his grief.
"For now I know," the voice proclaimed,
"You fear God, your faith unashamed.
Your son is spared, your heart is true,
And through your seed, all nations shall accrue."
Isaac, released, his life restored,
Yet the memory of that day forever scored.
A tale of faith, wild and raw,
Of love that obeys, despite the flaw.
For in that moment, on Moriah's peak,
Where the air was thick, and God seemed bleak,
A glimpse of another, a shadow so near,
Of a sacrifice greater, of a Son so dear.
But for now, the ram, the fire, the wood,
Were a testament that God is good.
Yet the shock remains, the awe, the fear,
Of a God who tests, and a faith held dear.

Abraham named that place Jehovah-Jireh,
The Lord will provide, in the highest lyre.
For there, on the mount, a story was penned,
Of faith unbroken, where fear must bend.
The Binding of Isaac, a tale wild and grim,
Of a God who calls, and the trust within.
But beyond the shock, the terror, the flame,
Is the truth of love, forever the same.

The Journey for a Bride

In the twilight of life, where the sands run thin,
Abraham pondered the promise within.
His son, Isaac, the heir of his line,
Must find a bride, by the hand of the Divine.
"Go to my homeland," Abraham decreed,
To his servant, faithful, in word and deed.
"Swear by the Lord, the God of the sky,
That you'll bring back a bride, from my kin, nearby."
The servant departed, with camels in train,
To the land of Nahor, across the vast plain.
He carried the hopes of a nation unborn,
To find a bride for the son who was sworn.
As the sun dipped low, in a foreign land,
He prayed by a well, with a trembling hand.
"O Lord of my master, guide me this day,
Show me the one, in Your chosen way."
Before the prayer faded into the air,
A maiden approached, with beauty so rare.
Rebekah her name, with kindness so sweet,
She offered him water, and the camels to treat.
A sign from above, the servant's heart soared,
For here was the answer, a gift from the Lord.
He placed a ring on her delicate hand,

DIVINE ECHOES: POEMS OF PROPHETS, FAITH, & REDEMPTION

A promise of union, a vow to stand.
Her family agreed, the blessing was given,
A journey of love, by the hand of heaven.
Rebekah departed, with joy in her eyes,
To meet her bridegroom, under Canaan's skies.
As they approached, in the evening's soft glow,
Isaac walked in the fields, where the breezes blow.
He lifted his eyes, and behold, she was there,
A vision of grace, beyond all compare.
Rebekah alighted, her heart in her chest,
Covered her face, in a gesture so blessed.
Isaac took her, with love so deep,
And the promise of God began to reap.
In the tent of his mother, Rebekah was laid,
And there their love, in faith, was portrayed.
Two lives entwined, by the will of the Lord,
A union of purpose, a future restored.
The servant returned, his mission complete,
With a tale of wonder, a story so sweet.
For in the journey, the prayer, the well,
Was the hand of God, where love would dwell.
Thus, Isaac and Rebekah, together they stood,
In the land of promise, as God had understood.
A covenant born in the faith of the old,
A story of love, forever retold.
In the quiet of the night, under stars so bright,
The legacy of Abraham took flight.
For in Genesis 24, the tale unfolds,
Of a love predestined, in the ancient molds.
So let it be known, from age to age,

The story of Isaac, on history's page.
A journey of faith, a bride, a son,
In the hands of God, two hearts were won.

The Brothers' Strife

In the womb of Rebekah, a struggle began,
Two nations at war, in the heart of one man.
Twins, yet divided, by destiny's hand,
Jacob and Esau, the heirs of the land.
Esau, the firstborn, with hair like the earth,
A hunter, a warrior, from the day of his birth.
Jacob, the younger, with cunning and grace,
Grasping the heel, in the ultimate race.
The birthright was Esau's, the blessing his claim,
But Jacob desired the fire of fame.
With stew as his weapon, he set the trap,
For a hungry Esau, caught in the gap.
"Sell me your birthright," Jacob did plead,
And Esau, in hunger, planted the seed.
A birthright for bread, a future for naught,
In that fateful exchange, Esau was caught.
But the story was deeper, more twisted and wild,
For a mother's love for her younger child.
Rebekah conspired, with a whisper so cold,
To steal the blessing, with deception bold.
Isaac, the father, old and blind,
Called Esau to him, with blessing in mind.
But Jacob, in skins, deceived his own kin,

And took what was Esau's, a terrible sin.
The blessing was given, the deed was done,
And Esau returned, to find the race won.
A cry of anguish, a roar of despair,
As Esau realized the theft laid bare.
"Is there no blessing for me, my father?" he wept,
But Isaac, in sorrow, the promise kept.
"You shall live by the sword, in the land of Edom,
And serve your brother, though you seek freedom."
Jacob fled, with fear in his heart,
For Esau's wrath tore him apart.
Years passed by, in a land afar,
But the memory of Esau left a scar.
Yet time can heal, and brothers can change,
As Jacob returned, with gifts to arrange.
He bowed before Esau, in the dust of the land,
But Esau embraced him, extending his hand.
No longer the hunter, no longer the heel,
But two men, brothers, who learned to heal.
The birthright, the blessing, the strife of old,
Melted away, as their story was told.
In the embrace of forgiveness, they found their peace,
And the wounds of the past began to cease.
For in the end, despite the pain,
Jacob and Esau were brothers again.
So remember the tale of the twins in the womb,
Of birthright and blessing, and destiny's loom.
For in the weaving of life's great plan,
Is the story of two brothers, and the heart of man.

The Tale of Jacob's Love

In the shadow of mountains, where the winds softly sigh,
Jacob journeyed alone, beneath the vast sky.
A fugitive of fate, with a heart full of dreams,
He wandered to Haran, where the light gently gleams.
By a well, he rested, weary and worn,
When a shepherdess approached, in the early morn.
Her eyes like the stars, her beauty so rare,
Jacob's heart leapt, as he stood unaware.
This was Rachel, the daughter of Laban,
A vision of grace in the morning sun.
Jacob's heart, once a wanderer's stone,
Began to beat for a love yet unknown.
With strength unbridled, he rolled the stone,
And watered her flock, his heart overthrown.
She ran to her father, the tale to tell,
Of a man by the well, under love's sweet spell.
Laban welcomed him in, with a cunning smile,
Yet Jacob's thoughts were with Rachel all the while.
"I will serve you seven years," he declared with pride,
"For your daughter Rachel, to be my bride."
The years flew by, like days in the sun,
For the love of Rachel, the race was run.
But on the night of the wedding, in the dim of the night,

LEAH NIFFHONDRO

A shadow crept in, and the dream took flight.
For Laban, with trickery, switched the brides,
And Jacob awoke with Leah by his side.
A cry of despair, a heart torn in two,
As the dawn revealed what the darkness knew.
But Laban, with craft, spoke words so smooth,
"Finish the week, and Rachel shall soothe.
Another seven years, for the love you desire,
And Rachel shall join you, as hearts conspire."
So Jacob toiled, with love in his soul,
For the bride he desired, his ultimate goal.
At last, she was his, the one he adored,
But the shadow of Leah forever scored.
Two sisters in a house, where love was divided,
Rachel, beloved, and Leah, derided.
Yet Leah bore sons, while Rachel's womb wept,
And Jacob's heart, with sorrow, was swept.
But love, in its depth, can grow through the pain,
As Jacob learned in this tangled domain.
For in Leah's eyes, there flickered a light,
Of a love unbidden, but steadfast in night.
And Rachel, though barren, held Jacob's heart,
A love so fierce, it tore him apart.
But in time, God remembered her tears,
And Joseph was born, dispelling the fears.
So Genesis 29, a tale wild and deep,
Of love and deception, of promises to keep.
Of a man who labored, for the love of his life,
Yet found himself bound by a double-edged knife.
For in the end, love's lesson was clear,

It weaves through the heart, both far and near.
In the house of Laban, where Jacob was tried,
Was the story of love, purified and tried.
So let this tale be remembered, for ages to come,
Of Jacob, Rachel, and Leah, as one.
For in their lives, a truth is revealed,
That love, in its fullness, can never be sealed.

The Dreamer's Betrayal

In the fields of Canaan, where the sun's light gleams,
There lived a young dreamer, with visions and dreams.
Joseph, the favored, the son of old age,
In a coat of many colors, his heart did engage.
But love so deep, like a double-edged sword,
Bred envy and hate, in his brothers' accord.
For each dream he shared, each vision he spoke,
Drove a wedge in their hearts, until brotherhood broke.
One night, he dreamed of sheaves in the field,
His brothers' sheaves bowed, their anger unsealed.
Then stars and the moon, in a vision so grand,
Bowed down to him, in the silence of sand.
"Shall you reign over us?" his brothers did cry,
Their hearts filled with spite, as they plotted nearby.
A hatred was born, so fierce and so cold,
In the shadow of love, betrayal took hold.
One day, Jacob sent Joseph to the fields far away,
To find his brothers, in the heat of the day.
But as they saw him, from afar he came,
A plot in their hearts, to erase his name.
"Here comes the dreamer," they whispered with scorn,
"Let's kill him now, and be rid of his thorn."
But Reuben, the eldest, with a heart still torn,

Said, "Shed no blood, throw him into the pit forlorn."
So they stripped him of his coat, that symbol of pride,
And cast him into a pit, dark and wide.
No water, no hope, in the darkness he lay,
While his brothers sat down, to eat and betray.
But then Judah spoke, with greed in his eyes,
"Why kill our brother, when we can rise?
Let's sell him to the Ishmaelites, who pass by this way,
And be rid of the dreamer, without blood to repay."
So for twenty pieces of silver, they sold their kin,
And watched as he was taken, his dreams now thin.
Bound and broken, Joseph was led,
To a land of strangers, where his dreams bled.
But the brothers took his coat, stained it with blood,
And brought it to Jacob, where grief like a flood,
Overwhelmed the old man, as he tore his clothes,
For the son he had lost, whom he deeply chose.
"My son is dead," Jacob wept in despair,
As the brothers stood silent, under the air.
But little did they know, in their hatred's dark plight,
That Joseph's dreams would still take flight.
In the land of Egypt, where he was sold as a slave,
A new story began, with a path yet to pave.
For the dreamer would rise, though now cast down,
From the depths of betrayal, he would wear the crown.
So Genesis 37, a chapter of pain,
Of a father's loss and a brother's gain.
But deep in the sorrow, beneath the deceit,
Is a tale of redemption, where dreams and fate meet.
For Joseph, the dreamer, though bruised and betrayed,

Would one day see his visions replayed.
In the heart of Egypt, where the river winds,
The dreamer's tale would redeem mankind.

The Temptation and Triumph

In the land of Egypt, far from his home,
Joseph stood alone, where dreams had flown.
Sold into slavery, stripped of his pride,
Yet within his heart, God's presence did abide.
In Potiphar's house, Joseph rose with grace,
A servant so faithful, in a foreign place.
His hands brought blessing, his work was pure,
In the house of his master, his heart was sure.
But beneath the surface, a storm would rise,
In the eyes of Potiphar's wife, deceitful and wise.
She cast her gaze on Joseph, with desire aflame,
And whispered seduction, calling his name.
"Lie with me, Joseph," she urged with a sigh,
But Joseph stood firm, with resolve in his eye.
"How could I do this, and sin against God?
Your husband trusts me, and I honor his rod."
Day after day, she pursued with intent,
But Joseph resisted, his will never bent.
Until one day, in the house alone,
She seized him by his cloak, her trap fully shown.
But Joseph fled, leaving his garment behind,
A man of integrity, with a steadfast mind.
Yet she cried out loud, twisting the tale,

Accusing the innocent, and watching him pale.
Potiphar returned, his anger alight,
And cast Joseph in prison, deep in the night.
But even in chains, Joseph stood tall,
For God was with him, through it all.
In the darkness of prison, where hope seemed thin,
Joseph found favor, even therein.
The keeper of the prison saw God in his life,
And placed in his hands, the keys to the strife.
Joseph's light shone, even in the gloom,
As he interpreted dreams, dispelling the doom.
For two of Pharaoh's men, once favored and high,
Found in Joseph's words, the truth that won't lie.
The cupbearer restored, the baker condemned,
Yet Joseph's name was forgotten, as time would bend.
Two long years passed, in the shadows and chains,
But Joseph's faith, through trials, remains.
Then Pharaoh dreamed, of famine and feast,
And called for the wise, from the greatest to the least.
But none could unravel the visions so strange,
Until the cupbearer remembered the name.
Joseph was summoned, from prison's deep cell,
To stand before Pharaoh, where destiny fell.
He spoke of the future, of seven years of plenty,
Followed by famine, with hunger aplenty.
Pharaoh was amazed, by the wisdom displayed,
And Joseph was exalted, his journey repaid.
From prisoner to prince, in the land of the Nile,
Joseph's dreams were fulfilled, after every trial.
In the heart of Egypt, where power and fame,

Joseph remained true, to the God of his name.
Through temptation and trials, through betrayal and pain,
He rose like the sun, after the rain.
Genesis 39, a tale of might,
Of a man who walked by faith, and not by sight.
For in the land of Egypt, where he was once bound,
Joseph found favor, and his dreams were crowned.

Chains of a Nation

Beneath the burning sun, where the Nile winds slow,
A people cried out, in the shadows of woe.
Israel, once cherished, now shackled in pain,
In the land of Egypt, where the tears fell like rain.
Once they had flourished, in Joseph's embrace,
But a new Pharaoh rose, with a hardened face.
He feared their numbers, their strength in the land,
So he bound them in chains, with an iron hand.
They toiled in the fields, in the blistering heat,
Their backs bent low, as their spirits beat.
Brick by brick, they built the throne,
For a king who knew not what their God had shown.
The lash of the whip, the curse of the slave,
Echoed through the valleys, where the Hebrews gave
Their sweat, their blood, to the stone and the sand,
As the years wore on, like a funeral band.
But deep in their hearts, a fire still burned,
A promise of old, that never had turned.
The God of their fathers, the God of their kin,
Would hear their cries, and deliver them again.
Yet the nights were long, and the days were grim,
As mothers wept for the children born slim.
For Pharaoh, in fear, decreed with dread,

DIVINE ECHOES: POEMS OF PROPHETS, FAITH, & REDEMPTION

That every Hebrew boy be cast into the river, dead.
But in the midst of the sorrow, a cry of defiance,
A mother's love, and a daring reliance.
She placed her child in a basket of reeds,
And set him adrift, where the river leads.
The baby was found, by the daughter of a king,
And Moses was raised, with the royal ring.
But his heart was torn, between two lands,
The cries of his people, the chains on their hands.
One day he saw, an Egyptian's cruel blow,
And in righteous anger, he struck down his foe.
He fled to the desert, with fear in his stride,
But God's voice found him, where he could not hide.
"Go back," said the Lord, with a flame in His breath,
"Set My people free, from the grip of death.
Tell Pharaoh, the tyrant, that My hand is strong,
And I will redeem them, from all that is wrong."
Moses returned, with Aaron by his side,
And the people of Israel, their fear set aside.
But Pharaoh's heart was as hard as stone,
And the plagues that followed made Egypt moan.
Blood in the rivers, and darkness at noon,
Hail from the heavens, and the firstborn's doom.
But in the land of Goshen, where the Hebrews cried,
The angel of death passed over, and life was supplied.
Then came the exodus, wild and free,
As the Red Sea parted, and the Hebrews could see
The chains that had bound them, now shattered and gone,
As they crossed to freedom, under the dawn.
Yet the memories lingered, of the years in the dust,

LEAH NIFFHONDRO

The taste of their tears, and the Pharaoh's unjust.
They carried the scars, of a slavery so deep,
But in their hearts, the promise they'd keep.
For Israel was born, in the crucible of pain,
A nation delivered, through fire and rain.
Their God had heard, their God had seen,
And through the wilderness, their path was keen.
So remember the chains, the sorrow, the night,
And the God who brought them into the light.
For in the story of Israel, a truth is unfurled,
That freedom is forged, in the furnace of the world.

The Cradle in the Nile

In the shadow of the tyrant's decree,
Where Egypt's sands kissed the Nile's soft plea,
A mother's heart, like a drum, did pound,
Her tears a river, her sobs the sound.
She held her child, a sacred flame,
An innocent spark in a world of shame.
Oh, how her soul was torn in two,
Between love's bond and what she knew.
The stars above, they seemed to weep,
As she placed her son in the waters deep.
The reeds whispered secrets, ancient and wise,
While she cried out to the silent skies.
"How can I let him drift away,
This fragile light, this break of day?"
But within her breast, hope took flight,
A desperate prayer in the dead of night.
The basket rocked with the river's sigh,
As angels watched with a tender eye.
The waters trembled, the current stilled,
For in this child, a fate was willed.
Pharaoh's daughter, with a heart unchained,
Found the boy where the reeds had strained.
A cry, a gasp, a mother's face,

LEAH NIFFHONDRO

In a princess's arms, a child found grace.
From sorrow's depths, a nation's cry,
Rose with the sun in the desert sky.
This child of water, born of strife,
Would soon awaken a people's life.
The wind it howled, the heavens roared,
As destiny struck with a double-edged sword.
For in this babe, both joy and pain,
The storm that would break the tyrant's reign.
Oh, mother of Moses, with eyes so wild,
You birthed a prophet, a savior, a child.
Your tears became the Nile's great song,
Echoing freedom, fierce and long.
So sing, oh desert, of the life once cast,
In waters deep where fate was vast.
For in that cradle, hope was born,
And the chains of the past were forever torn.

DIVINE ECHOES: POEMS OF PROPHETS, FAITH, & REDEMPTION

Flames of the Unseen Voice

In the barren heart of a wilderness land,
Where the desert winds carve tales in sand,
A shepherd walked with burdened stride,
His past a shadow, his future denied.
The sun, a fierce and relentless eye,
Watched as he passed the mountains high.
But in the silence, a whisper grew,
A voice that the world never knew.
He turned, his breath caught in his chest,
For there it blazed, a fire undressed—
A bush aflame, yet unconsumed,
A holy fire in a desert tomb.
The flames danced wild, yet gentle too,
A paradox of the sacred view.
Moses, with trembling hands and feet,
Felt the pulse of the earth's heartbeat.
A voice like thunder, yet soft as rain,
Called out his name, his life to claim.
"Moses, Moses," the fire sighed,
And in those flames, all fears died.
"Take off your sandals, this ground is pure,
For I am the God you once knew sure—
The God of your fathers, of Abraham's name,

DIVINE ECHOES: POEMS OF PROPHETS, FAITH, & REDEMPTION

Of Isaac's faith and Jacob's flame."
Moses, trembling, dared not see,
The burning truth of the mystery.
"Who am I, that I should go?
I am but a man, broken, low."
But the voice within the fire's embrace,
Spoke with a power, a boundless grace.
"I AM WHO I AM," the flames declared,
A name that all existence bared.
"Go now, speak to the Pharaoh's might,
For in your hand is freedom's light.
With every step, I shall be near,
To turn your weakness into fear."
The fire burned with purpose bright,
Illuminating the endless night.
Moses felt his spirit blaze,
A torch of hope in a world of haze.
His doubts were ashes in that holy place,
His fears consumed by the divine embrace.
He left the bush, his path made clear,
With the fire's voice ringing in his ear.
For in that desert, by the flame's decree,
A shepherd became a prophet free.
The burning bush, forevermore,
A symbol of the holy war.
Against oppression, against the chains,
Against the darkness where evil reigns.
Moses, chosen, with eyes alight,
Walked into Egypt's darkest night.
With the fire's power in his soul,

He led his people to their goal.
For the bush that burned with unyielding flame,
Ignited a legacy in God's own name.

Wrath of the Nile: The Tenfold Cry

The Nile, once a river of life,
Turned red as blood, the color of strife.
A crimson curse, a silent scream,
As Egypt's heart unraveled its dream.
Fishermen wept on the banks of despair,
As the life in the waters faded to air.
Oh, Pharaoh, stubborn in pride,
Could you not see the wrath at your side?
Then rose the frogs, in a green wave of dread,
Leaping from beds, from table to bread.
They croaked the truth, in every ear,
But still, the Pharaoh refused to hear.
In every corner, they echoed the plea,
"Let my people go, let them be free."
Yet the king's heart hardened, cold as stone,
And Egypt was left to suffer alone.
Lice like dust, they swarmed the land,
A biting plague, by God's command.
From the brows of slaves to the crowns of kings,
None were spared the torment it brings.
The priests in their temples, powerless and weak,
Knew in their hearts what the lice would speak.
But Pharaoh stood firm, his will like steel,

Blind to the pain that his people feel.
The beasts of the field, they roared in the night,
As wild things turned on Egypt in fright.
The flocks and herds, once Egypt's pride,
Fell under the curse, their lifeblood denied.
The land grew silent, a graveyard's breath,
As Pharaoh ignored the signs of death.
For every beast that fell in vain,
Was a cry for freedom, a cry of pain.
Then boils erupted, on flesh and skin,
A burning plague, a mark of sin.
The cries of the people filled the air,
As disease spread with no one to care.
Even the priests, with their sacred oils,
Could not escape these painful toils.
But Pharaoh's heart, cold and cruel,
Ignored the suffering, played the fool.
The heavens darkened, the skies turned black,
Hail fell like stones in a fierce attack.
Fire and ice, in a deadly dance,
Struck down the crops, left nothing to chance.
The earth shook under the weight of despair,
As Pharaoh refused to answer the prayer.
"Let my people go," the winds did wail,
But still, Pharaoh's heart did not quail.
Then locusts came in a ravenous swarm,
Stripping the land, leaving it torn.
Fields of green turned to barren dust,
As every plant crumbled into rust.
The people wept, their stomachs bare,

While Pharaoh ignored their desperate prayer.
For every leaf that the locusts consumed,
Was a hope destroyed, a dream entombed.
Darkness fell, a palpable gloom,
Three days of night, like a silent tomb.
The sun, ashamed, hid its face,
As Egypt stumbled in this dark embrace.
The light was gone, the hope was lost,
And yet Pharaoh refused to count the cost.
In the silence of that endless night,
The people trembled in fear and fright.
But the final blow, the tenth, the worst,
A scream in the night, a nation cursed.
The firstborn fell, from prince to slave,
Each breath snatched by the hand of the grave.
A mother's wail, a father's cry,
As every household said goodbye.
Pharaoh's heart, broken at last,
Knew the cost of holding fast.
And so the people, once bound in chains,
Walked out of Egypt in freedom's name.
The plagues, a testament of power and might,
A battle waged in the darkest night.
For every tear, for every pain,
Was a step towards breaking the reign.
The wrath of the Nile, the tenfold cry,
Brought down a kingdom, raised hopes high.
For in the end, the message was clear:
No tyrant can stand when God is near.
The plagues, wild and full of emotion,

LEAH NIFFHONDRO

Were the birth pangs of a nation's devotion.
And as they walked through the parted sea,
They knew the price of their liberty.

DIVINE ECHOES: POEMS OF PROPHETS, FAITH, & REDEMPTION

47

Blood on the Doorpost: The Passover Night

In the depths of night, when shadows creep,
And the world is hushed in restless sleep,
A whisper moved through the Hebrew camp,
A secret fire, a guiding lamp.
"Tonight," they said, "is the night of dread,
When the angel of death shall be widespread."
But in this night, a promise was born,
In the blood of a lamb, on a doorpost worn.
A mark of faith, a covenant signed,
That life would triumph, and death would be blind.
Each family gathered, with trembling hands,
As the lamb was slain by divine commands.
The blood, it flowed, a crimson tide,
Staining the wood where life would hide.
The father's hand, steady but pale,
Marked the threshold with the holy grail.
In silence, they waited, hearts beating fast,
As the dread of the night would soon be cast.
The moon hung low, an eye of despair,
As death's cold wind swept through the air.
It passed by homes with the blood-stained door,
But entered others with a silent roar.

DIVINE ECHOES: POEMS OF PROPHETS, FAITH, & REDEMPTION

From palace high to the humble shed,
The firstborn fell, the breath of the dead.
A mother's cry pierced the starless sky,
A nation's grief, a desperate why.
But in the homes where the blood was bright,
The children slept, untouched by night.
The angel passed, his scythe held low,
For the mark of the lamb made his power slow.
Through Egypt's streets, the wailing grew,
As Pharaoh's heart finally knew—
That no power or might, no earthly throne,
Could stand against the power shown.
He called for Moses, his voice a quake,
"Take your people, before I break."
And so they left, in the dawn's first light,
A people reborn from the darkest night.
The bread they carried, unrisen, flat,
A symbol of haste, of a journey at that.
For there was no time to linger or stay,
Freedom called, they must away.
The blood on the doorpost, a sign so pure,
Marked the night when life was secure.
A covenant sealed in the lamb's own blood,
A promise fulfilled in a holy flood.
For every drop that stained the wood,
Was a pledge from God, a bond that stood.
Passover night, a story of grace,
Of a people redeemed, a chosen race.
It echoes still, in every prayer,
A reminder that God is always there.

LEAH NIFFHONDRO

For in the blood, and in the bread,
We remember the night when death was shed.
Oh, Passover, night of might,
When darkness trembled at the sight—
Of a people marked by a sacred hand,
Led by God to the promised land.
For the angel of death, with his shadowed wing,
Could not withstand the power of the King.

The Path Through the Fury: Crossing the Red Sea

Beneath the heavens, heavy with dread,
A people fled where hope was thread.
The night was thick with fear and flight,
As they ran from chains into the night.
Behind them thundered a chariot's roar,
Pharaoh's wrath, a vengeful score.
Their hearts pounded with every stride,
But there was no place to run or hide.
The sea before them, vast and cold,
A liquid wall, a story untold.
Behind them, death in armor clad,
The slaves now free, but fearfully mad.
Children cried, mothers clung tight,
To the dream of freedom, born in night.
But how could they cross, this watery grave,
When Pharaoh's army sought to enslave?
Moses, his staff gripped firm in hand,
Stood by the shore, where sea meets land.
His voice rose up, a trembling plea,
"Fear not! Stand still and see!"
He raised his staff with hands of flame,
And called on God's unspoken name.

Then the wind, fierce and wild, did blow,
As the sea began to writhe and flow.
The waters heaved, then split in two,
A path of fear and faith did brew.
On either side, the walls stood tall,
A liquid fortress, ready to fall.
But through the middle, a path of dry,
A miracle stretched beneath the sky.
With hearts aflame, yet trembling still,
They stepped into the Creator's will.
Through the corridor of swirling waves,
They marched as free men, no longer slaves.
But with each step, the waters roared,
A primal scream, a call ignored.
Would this path hold, would they survive,
Or would they perish, barely alive?
The wind it howled, the sea did seethe,
As every breath was hard to breathe.
The children's cries were drowned by the sound,
Of crashing waves and thunder unbound.
But Moses led, with eyes of steel,
And in his gaze, they could feel—
The power of faith, the strength of trust,
That in God's hands, they were just.
As the last of the Hebrews crossed the sand,
Pharaoh's army reached the land.
They charged into the parted sea,
Certain of their victory.
But as they raced with death's own grin,
The sea began to close back in.

The walls of water, tall as skies,
Fell with a fury, drowned the cries.
Chariots crumbled, horses screamed,
The end of Egypt's power, it seemed.
The sea returned to its restless state,
And swallowed whole the army's fate.
On the distant shore, the Hebrews stood,
Their hearts a storm, their eyes like wood.
They watched the sea, now calm, now still,
And felt the rush of freedom's thrill.
But in that thrill, a sorrow too,
For the cost of freedom, they now knew.
The waves that saved, also did kill,
And the taste of death lingered still.
Yet in that mix of joy and pain,
They felt a strength they couldn't explain.
For they had seen the waters part,
And felt the pulse of God's own heart.
They sang a song of wild release,
Of chains broken and newfound peace.
But in their voices, wild and free,
Echoed the sorrow of the sea.
For freedom's price is never light,
It's born in struggle, pain, and might.
The Red Sea closed, but left behind,
A story etched in every mind.
A path through fury, wild and wide,
Where faith and fear walked side by side.
And in that crossing, they were reborn,
A people freed, but not yet worn.

LEAH NIFFHONDRO

For the sea had shown them, deep and true,
The power of God in all they do.
And as they marched to the desert's breath,
They knew they'd passed through life and death.
With hearts still racing, but spirits high,
They walked beneath a freedomed sky.

The Whisper of Dawn: The Foretelling of Christ

In the stillness of night, when stars held their breath,
And the world lay hushed in a dream of death,
A whisper came, like a breeze through the trees,
A promise of hope, carried on the seas.
The heavens stirred with a sacred sound,
As prophecy moved across the ground.
In the courts of heaven, the angels stood,
A hush fell over the celestial brood.
For the voice of God, with thunderous grace,
Spoke of a plan to redeem the race.
"Prepare," He said, "for the time draws near,
When light shall break through the darkness here."
The prophets of old, with vision keen,
Had glimpsed this day in their sacred dream.
Isaiah cried out with eyes aflame,
"Unto us a child shall come, bearing God's name.
A virgin shall conceive, pure and bright,
And the world shall be filled with holy light."
In Nazareth's town, so humble and small,
An angel descended with a silent call.
To a maiden pure, with heart so mild,
He spoke of the coming of God's own child.

"Fear not, Mary, for you are blessed,
Among all women, you are caressed
By God's own hand, chosen to bear,
The Savior of all, the answer to prayer."
Mary trembled, but her spirit soared,
As she bowed her head to the angel's word.
"Behold the handmaid of the Lord," she cried,
"Let it be to me as you have implied."
And in that moment, the world's fate turned,
As the fire of God within her burned.
Across the land, in a temple's hall,
An old priest stood, answering the call.
Gabriel came with a message clear,
To Zechariah, whose heart held fear.
"Your barren wife shall bear a son,
A prophet's voice, to announce the One.
He will go before the Lord most high,
To prepare the way, for the King draws nigh."
And in the hills of Bethlehem's plain,
The shepherds watched, in the cold and rain.
The stars above seemed to shine more bright,
As they sensed the coming of holy light.
For in the heavens, a choir did sing,
Of the coming birth of a newborn King.
The wise men far, with knowledge deep,
Read the skies, while others sleep.
A star arose, a sign divine,
Pointing to where the Savior would shine.
They packed their gifts, with hearts aglow,
To find the child the heavens show.

LEAH NIFFHONDRO

The earth itself seemed to hold its breath,
As it awaited the birth, the end of death.
For in every corner, in every heart,
The prophecy burned like a sacred art.
A King would come, in humble guise,
To open the blind and awaken the wise.
The birth of Jesus, foretold with grace,
Was the dawn of hope for the human race.
For in that night, so still, so deep,
The world awoke from its endless sleep.
And the light that shone in Bethlehem's stall,
Was the light of love, the greatest of all.
So let the heavens and earth proclaim,
The birth foretold, in God's own name.
For unto us, a child is born,
And with Him, a new world is sworn.
The angels sing, the prophets rejoice,
For in Jesus, we find our voice.

DIVINE ECHOES: POEMS OF PROPHETS, FAITH, & REDEMPTION

The Birth of Light: A King in a Manger

In the stillness of night, when all seemed lost,
And the world was bound in winter's frost,
A star ignited the heavens wide,
A beacon of hope, a cosmic tide.
The skies, once dark, now blazed with fire,
As angels sang with holy desire.
For on this night, in Bethlehem's glow,
The Savior was born, all hearts to know.
In a humble stable, by beasts surrounded,
The cries of a child in the night resounded.
Not in a palace, with splendor and gold,
But in the arms of a virgin, the story was told.
Mary, with eyes of wonder and grace,
Held in her arms the world's new face.
The breath of heaven in a newborn's sigh,
A promise of peace, a holy cry.
Shepherds in fields, with hearts of awe,
Heard the news that the angels saw.
"Fear not," they sang, "for joy we bring,
The birth of a child, a heavenly King.
In David's town, in a manger low,
Lies the One whom all shall know.
Go now, and see this wondrous sight,

The birth of the world's eternal light."
They ran with haste through the night's embrace,
To gaze upon the infant's face.
And there they knelt, in reverent fear,
As heaven's joy drew ever near.
This child, so small, yet full of might,
Held the power to banish night.
For in his hands, the fate of man,
In his heart, the divine plan.
Wise men from the east, with treasures rare,
Followed the star through the desert air.
They came to bow before the throne,
Not of gold, but of flesh and bone.
With gifts of myrrh, frankincense, and gold,
They worshiped the King, as prophets foretold.
For in this child, both man and divine,
The world's redemption began to shine.
The birth of Jesus, more than a tale,
Is the dawn of love that will never fail.
In this moment, time stood still,
As heaven and earth bent to God's will.
The chains of sin began to break,
As the light of the world started to wake.
No power of man, no earthly king,
Could stop the song the angels sing.
For in this birth, the truth was sown,
That God himself had come down, grown,
To walk among us, to share our pain,
To lift the lost, to break the chain.
The Word made flesh, the light of grace,

LEAH NIFFHONDRO

In Jesus, we see God's own face.
A love so fierce, a love so pure,
In this child, our hope secure.
This birth, a seed of heaven's plan,
Would grow to save the soul of man.
Through cross and grave, through death's dark night,
This child would lead us to the light.
For unto us, this gift was given,
A bridge from earth to highest heaven.
The birth of Jesus, a story old,
Yet ever new, its power untold.
So let the earth rejoice and sing,
For in this child, we find our King.
The humble birth, the starry night,
The dawn of love, the end of plight.
In Jesus' birth, the world's reborn,
A light that shines through every storm.
For in that manger, low and wild,
God's love was born in a humble child.

The Shepherds' Night: A Vision of Angels

On a night so still, beneath the sky's vast dome,
Where shepherds watched their flocks roam,
The world seemed hushed, wrapped in sleep,
As the stars above their vigil keep.
The fire flickered, the night was deep,
And silence held the world in its keep.
Yet in the darkness, a light began to grow,
A heavenly radiance, a soft, golden glow.
The shepherds, humble, with eyes wide in awe,
Saw the night split by a sight they never saw.
The heavens opened, the skies unfurled,
As angels descended, bright wings swirled.
A multitude, a heavenly host,
Singing praises to the utmost.
"Glory to God," their voices soared,
"Peace on earth," they all implored.
Their song was a river, a rushing stream,
Of joy and hope, a living dream.
The shepherds, frozen in holy fear,
Felt heaven's song fill the atmosphere.
Their hearts raced, their spirits soared,
As the message of the angels poured.

LEAH NIFFHONDRO

"Fear not," the angel's voice was clear,
"For we bring good news, so draw near.
In Bethlehem, this very night,
A Savior is born, the world's true light.
Wrapped in cloth, in a manger laid,
The Son of God, the price is paid.
Go now, and see this wondrous sight,
The birth of a King, the end of night."
The shepherds, with hearts ablaze,
Left their flocks, their fields, their ways.
They ran with joy through the night's embrace,
To see the child, to behold His face.
The stars above, a guiding beam,
Led them on, as in a dream.
They found Him there, as the angels said,
In a manger, where cattle fed.
Mary and Joseph, with eyes of grace,
Welcomed them to the holy place.
The shepherds knelt, their voices stilled,
As the promise of heaven was fulfilled.
Tears of wonder filled their eyes,
As they beheld the world's surprise.
A child so small, yet full of might,
The Savior born on this silent night.
The angels' song still in their ears,
A melody that calmed their fears.
They left the stable, hearts transformed,
To spread the news of the Savior born.
Their voices echoed in the night,
As they proclaimed the wondrous sight.

"The King is born, the Christ has come,
Rejoice, rejoice, for God's will is done!"
The shepherds' night, a night of awe,
Where heaven's glory, they clearly saw.
For in that field, beneath the stars,
They witnessed the breaking of heaven's bars.
A bridge was formed, a path was made,
In the birth of a King, our fears allayed.
The angels sang, the shepherds heard,
The world was changed by a simple word.
For on that night, so long and deep,
The world awoke from its ancient sleep.
The shepherds' night, forever bright,
A beacon of hope, a guiding light.

The Magi's Journey: A Star's Guiding Light

From the lands where the desert meets the sky,
Where the sands are vast and the winds do sigh,
Three wise men gazed at the night's expanse,
Their hearts are entranced by a star's bright dance.
In silence, they watched as it rose so high,
A beacon of hope in the midnight sky.
It whispered secrets of a King to be born,
A light in the darkness, a world reborn.
With treasures in hand and hearts set ablaze,
They mounted their camels to begin their praise.
Through desert winds and mountains steep,
They journeyed far with faith to keep.
Their minds were filled with ancient lore,
Prophecies told from days of yore.
They followed the star, a heavenly sign,
To find the child, the divine design.
The nights were long, the days were harsh,
But the star led on through the endless march.
Their journey was one of faith and fire,
Of seeking the truth, of holy desire.
Through valleys deep and rivers wide,
They pressed on, with the star as their guide.

For they knew in their hearts, beyond all reason,
That this was the dawn of a sacred season.
At last, they came to Bethlehem's gate,
Where the star shone bright, its light innate.
Their hearts beat fast, their breaths were still,
As they approached the house on the hill.
Inside, they found the child divine,
The Savior of all, in human sign.
Mary, with a mother's grace,
Watched as the Magi beheld His face.
With trembling hands, they laid their gifts,
Gold, frankincense, and myrrh, in shifts.
The gold for a King, with power untold,
The frankincense for a priest, pure and bold.
The myrrh, a bitter symbol of sacrifice,
Foreshadowing the ultimate price.
They knelt in reverence, their souls laid bare,
Before the child who would one day bear
The sins of the world, the weight of man,
In a plan so divine, no mind could span.
Tears filled their eyes, their hearts overflowed,
As they felt the presence of God bestowed.
The room was filled with a holy light,
As they worshiped the child, the world's new sight.
For in this humble, quiet space,
They saw the dawn of amazing grace.
The Magi knew, as they stood in awe,
They had witnessed the fulfillment of the law.
With hearts full of joy, yet tinged with sorrow,
They knew that this child held the morrow.

His life would bring both joy and pain,
A King who would die, yet rise again.
They left the house, their spirits high,
With the star still shining in the sky.
For they had seen the face of God,
In a humble child, on the earth He trod.
Their journey home was filled with peace,
For they had found the soul's release.
The star had led them to the light,
That would shine through every night.
And as they traveled back through the land,
They spread the news of God's grand plan.
The Magi's visit, a tale of grace,
Of seeking and finding God's own face.
For in that moment, so wild, so grand,
The world was changed by a child's hand.
The Magi's journey, a testament true,
Of the power of faith to see us through.
And in their story, we find our way,
To seek the light, to kneel and pray.
For the star still shines in the hearts of men,
Leading us to Bethlehem again.

The Presentation: A Child of Light in the Temple's Halls

In days of old, when time stood still,
And sacred rites the hearts did fill,
A mother pure, with babe in arm,
Did journey forth to the temple's charm.
With Joseph true, her steadfast guide,
They walked with grace, with faith as guide.
The temple, grand with pillars high,
Rose toward the vast, eternal sky.
Its halls were hushed, its lamps aglow,
As Mary entered, soft and slow.
The child she bore, the holy light,
Shone like a star in the deepest night.
Simeon, aged, with eyes that yearn'd,
For this one day his soul had turn'd.
Long had he prayed, long had he wept,
In God's own promise, his trust was kept.
The Spirit's voice had whispered clear,
"That thou shalt see the Lord draw near."
With trembling hands and heart afire,
He saw the child, his soul's desire.
"Now lettest thou thy servant go,"
He whispered soft, with eyes aglow.

"For thy eyes have seen the saving grace,
In this child's pure, unblemished face."
A light to lighten Gentile's night,
The glory of Israel, burning bright.
This babe, so small, yet full of might,
Would pierce the dark with heaven's light.
Simeon's tears did freely flow,
As he blessed the child, both high and low.
Anna, prophetess, wise and old,
Did see the babe, as scriptures told.
With joy she spoke to all who sought,
The redemption that this child brought.
For she had waited long and true,
To see the dawn, the morning dew.
But lo, a sword shall pierce thy soul,
To Mary, words of bitter toll.
For this child shall rise and fall,
The sign for many, the call for all.
And in His path, both joy and pain,
Shall mingle like the sun and rain.
Yet fear not, for the light shall shine,
Through every dark, through every sign.
This holy child, in temple's keep,
Shall wake the world from endless sleep.
A Savior born, in humble guise,
To open the blind and heal the wise.
So in the temple's hallowed hall,
Was seen the hope, the end of thrall.
For Jesus, Lord of earth and sky,
Was offered here, for all to die.

His life, a sacrifice so pure,
To cleanse the world, to make it sure.
And thus the tale, in olden time,
Was sung in verse, was told in rhyme.
Of how the Christ, in temple bright,
Was shown to be the world's true light.
A story old, yet ever new,
Of love divine, of faith so true.
For in that temple, on that day,
The world did see the narrow way.
Through Him, the gate, the shepherd true,
The light of God was given you.
So let us sing, in voices bold,
The tale of Christ, forever told.

The Flight to Egypt: A Journey of Shadows and Light

In the dead of night, when stars were dim,
And the world was hushed by a silent hymn,
A warning came on angel's breath,
Of danger near, of looming death.
Joseph stirred from his sleep so deep,
As heaven's voice did softly creep.
"Rise, take the child and Mary fair,
And flee to Egypt's distant air."
The night was still, the world asleep,
But Joseph knew the path was steep.
With haste he rose, his heart aflame,
To protect the child of heaven's name.
Mary, with eyes of quiet trust,
Gathered the babe, as all she must.
For in her arms, the Savior lay,
The light of dawn, the hope of day.
Through the winding streets of Bethlehem,
They slipped away, like a hidden gem.
The shadows cast by the moon's faint light,
Guided their steps through the silent night.
The cold wind whispered of dangers near,
Yet faith was stronger than any fear.

LEAH NIFFHONDRO

Across the desert, wide and vast,
They journeyed far, they traveled fast.
The sands of time beneath their feet,
Bore witness to their quiet retreat.
Through every dune, through every hill,
The promise of God was with them still.
The sun arose with a fiery blaze,
But in their hearts, no fear could raise.
For Egypt loomed, a land of old,
A refuge safe, as was foretold.
The palm trees swayed in the desert's breath,
As they crossed the threshold of life and death.
Herod's wrath, a tempest fierce,
Could not the holy child pierce.
For in Egypt's arms, they found their rest,
A sanctuary, a place so blessed.
The cries of Rachel, far away,
Were silenced by the break of day.
And in that foreign, distant land,
The child grew strong, by God's own hand.
The land of pyramids, of ancient lore,
Held the light that the world would soon adore.
In Egypt's shadow, the dawn took root,
For salvation's tree would bear its fruit.
Yet Egypt's land was not their home,
For soon the call would bid them roam.
When Herod's death brought peace anew,
The angel spoke with words so true.
"Return," he said, "to Israel's heart,
For now the danger shall depart."

So back they went, the way they came,
With faith as strong, with hearts the same.
But in their flight, a tale was spun,
Of God's protection, of what was done.
The flight to Egypt, a journey wild,
Preserved the life of Heaven's child.
For in that night, so dark, so deep,
The Lord did watch, the Lord did keep.
The Son of Man, in swaddling clothes,
Escaped the grasp of earthly foes.
And in their flight, a promise shone,
That God would never leave His own.
So let us remember, in times of fear,
That God is always, always near.
For in the flight to Egypt's land,
We see the work of His mighty hand.
A story of love, a story of grace,
That in our hearts, finds its place.

The Boy in the Temple: A Light Among Scholars

In the heart of Jerusalem, bustling and grand,
Where wisdom's echoes filled the land,
A boy of twelve, with eyes so bright,
Walked through the gates, bathed in light.
His steps were sure, his gaze serene,
A child, yet more, with purpose keen.
The temple's courts, with marble gleam,
Held the echoes of a timeless dream.
Priests and scholars, draped in white,
Gathered there in holy rite.
But amidst the scrolls and ancient lore,
A voice was heard, unseen before.
The boy sat down with scholars wise,
Questions burning in his eyes.
He spoke with grace, with truth so deep,
That even the elders ceased to speak.
For in his words, a fire did burn,
A wisdom that made their spirits yearn.
"Who is this child?" the rabbis mused,
With every answer, more confused.
His voice, like honey, smooth and clear,
Drew them close, yet filled with fear.

For every question they did pose,
He answered with a light that glows.
The prophets' words, the ancient songs,
He knew them all, to whom they belong.
He spoke of Isaiah, of David's psalms,
Of God's great plan, of soothing calms.
The elders marveled, their hearts ablaze,
Caught in the spell of the child's gaze.
But as the hours slipped away,
His parents sought him in dismay.
Mary, anxious, her heart a storm,
Found him there, so wise, so warm.
"Son, why hast thou treated us so?
Thy father and I, in sorrow, do know."
With eyes so gentle, yet filled with might,
He answered them in the temple's light,
"Know ye not that I must be,
About my Father's work, so free?"
His words, a mystery, so profound,
Yet in them, truth was surely found.
For in that moment, time stood still,
As heaven's plan began to fill.
The boy, no ordinary child,
Was God's own Son, pure and mild.
In the temple's halls, so grand, so old,
A new story was quietly told.
He returned with them to Nazareth,
In humble silence, free of breath.
But in his heart, the fire remained,
The knowledge of what must be gained.

LEAH NIFFHONDRO

And as he grew, in strength and grace,
The world awaited his embrace.
For that day in the temple's court,
Was more than just a childhood sport.
It was the dawn of a new light,
A spark that would banish night.
The boy Jesus, in wisdom's place,
Showed the world a glimpse of grace.
A light among scholars, a child of God,
Whose path on earth the angels trod.
The boy in the temple, young yet wise,
Held the key to heaven's skies.
And in that moment, the world could see,
The promise of what was yet to be.

DIVINE ECHOES: POEMS OF PROPHETS, FAITH, & REDEMPTION

The Voice in the Wilderness: John's Sweet Call

In the quiet dawn, where the desert lies,
Beneath the expanse of endless skies,
A voice arose, soft yet strong,
A melody ancient, a timeless song.
John, the herald, with purpose clear,
Came forth to speak, for all to hear.
Clothed in camel's hair, with belt of leather,
He braved the wild, in every weather.
His diet simple, locusts and honey,
Yet his words were richer than gold or money.
For in his heart, a fire burned bright,
A calling divine, a guiding light.
"Prepare ye the way," he cried aloud,
"Make straight the paths, before the crowd.
For one comes after, greater than I,
The sandals of whom I am unworthy to tie.
Repent, repent, for the kingdom is near,
The Lord of all is drawing near."
The river Jordan, a flowing grace,
Became the stage, the holy place.
As people came from near and far,
Drawn by the light of a heavenly star.

DIVINE ECHOES: POEMS OF PROPHETS, FAITH, & REDEMPTION

John baptized with water clear,
A sign of cleansing, a heart sincere.
But as he spoke, his eyes did shine,
With visions of the Lamb divine.
"For I baptize with water pure,
But He shall come, with Spirit sure.
A fire will burn, a wind will blow,
In His presence, all shall know."
The crowds were moved, their hearts reborn,
As John prepared them for the morn.
The dawn of Christ, the Savior's day,
Was heralded in John's sweet way.
With every word, with every call,
He paved the road, he raised the hall.
And in the wilderness, where shadows fell,
John's voice became a sacred bell.
Ringing out through time and space,
Proclaiming the coming of God's own grace.
His message simple, yet profound,
In every heart, it did resound.
For in those days, so long ago,
John prepared the way for the light to show.
The tender shoot, the root of Jesse,
Would soon emerge, the world to bless ye.
And in the Jordan's flowing stream,
He baptized the One of whom he'd dream.
John's task was sweet, his purpose clear,
To ready the world for the One so dear.
And as he preached with humble might,
The path was set, the world made right.

For in his words, the truth did play,
As John the Baptist prepared the way.

The Baptism of Light: The Jordan's Holy Tide

In the stillness of the morning's grace,
When the sun first kissed the earth's soft face,
The Jordan flowed, serene and wide,
A river of hope, a sacred guide.
And there, on its banks, with hearts aglow,
The people gathered, their faith to show.
John, the Baptist, with eyes of fire,
Stood in the water, his voice a choir.
He called to the crowd, "Repent, be clean,
For the kingdom of God shall soon be seen."
But as he spoke, the skies did part,
And a holy presence filled each heart.
For down the path, so humble, so mild,
Came Jesus, the Father's beloved child.
His steps were sure, His purpose clear,
As He approached, the people drew near.
John's heart leapt, with joy and awe,
For in this moment, he clearly saw.
"Behold the Lamb, the sinless one,
The light of the world, God's own Son.
I am not worthy to untie His shoe,
Yet He comes now, the promise true."

But Jesus, with a gentle nod,
Stepped into the waters, kissed by God.
"Baptize me, John," He softly said,
"To fulfill all righteousness, as we've read."
John's hands, trembling, yet filled with grace,
Lowered the Savior in that holy place.
The water closed around His form,
A symbol of death, the end of the storm.
But as He rose, from the waters deep,
The heavens awoke from their ancient sleep.
The sky was rent with a mighty sound,
As the Spirit of God came swirling down.
A dove descended, pure and bright,
Resting on Jesus, bathed in light.
Then from above, a voice did ring,
The voice of God, of Heaven's King.
"This is My Son, in whom I delight,
My beloved, My joy, My purest light."
The earth stood still, the waters calmed,
As heaven and earth were sweetly charmed.
The people trembled, with hearts anew,
For in that moment, the truth they knew.
The Lamb of God, the chosen one,
Had come to save, to heal, to shun—
The darkness of sin, the shadows of night,
To bring the world into the light.
The Jordan's flow, forever changed,
By the power of God, so unrestrained.
For in that river, pure and wide,
The Savior's mission was sanctified.

DIVINE ECHOES: POEMS OF PROPHETS, FAITH, & REDEMPTION

A journey begun, a path so steep,
That even angels would stand and weep.
The baptism of Jesus, a holy start,
A moment that stirred the world's heart.
For in those waters, love was poured,
And the heavens opened, to praise the Lord.
The Son of Man, the Son of God,
Began His walk on the earth we trod.
And as the dove did soar on high,
The promise of hope filled the sky.
For in that baptism, we all were claimed,
By the grace of God, forever named.
The river's song, a sacred hymn,
Echoed the truth, the light within.
So let us remember, in faith and love,
The day when heaven smiled above.
When Jesus stepped into the Jordan's tide,
And God's own voice was glorified.
For in that moment, pure and bright,
The world was touched by eternal light.

In the Wilderness: The Temptation of Christ

In the wilderness, where the shadows lie,
Beneath a burning, relentless sky,
The Savior walked, alone and still,
Led by the Spirit, by the Father's will.
For forty days, with no bread to eat,
He wandered in hunger, with blistered feet.
Yet His resolve, like iron, was strong,
As He faced the trial that would come along.
The desert winds howled, fierce and wild,
But in His heart, a strength beguiled.
The stones, like teeth, underfoot did grind,
Yet no complaint crossed His mind.
His lips were dry, His body worn,
But in His spirit, a fire was born.
For He knew the hour was drawing near,
When the tempter's voice would soon appear.
And then, like a whisper, soft yet clear,
The devil approached, with a voice to hear.
A serpent's smile, a cunning guise,
He looked into Jesus' steadfast eyes.
"If Thou be the Son of God," he said,
"Turn these stones to loaves of bread.

Satisfy Thy hunger, break Thy fast,
For who could blame Thee, at long last?"
But Jesus stood, with gaze so bright,
And answered the tempter's subtle slight,
"Man shall not live by bread alone,
But by every word from the Father's throne."
The air grew tense, the devil frowned,
His next move silent, but the earth felt it pound.
In a moment, they stood on the temple's height,
The city below, bathed in night.
The devil's voice, like a serpent's hiss,
Spoke words laced with poison's kiss.
"If Thou be the Son of God, then leap,
For angels shall keep Thee, safe in sleep.
It is written, after all, is it not?
That He shall bear Thee, lest Thy foot be caught?"
But Jesus, calm as a mountain's stone,
Looked down with eyes that shone,
"Thou shalt not tempt the Lord thy God,"
He spoke with a voice that angels laud.
The tempter's face, a shadowed frown,
Began to darken, to drag him down.
But Satan, cunning, would not yield,
He took Jesus to a mountain's field.
The world lay spread in splendor bright,
Every kingdom, every light.
"All this," he said, with voice like silk,
"I'll give to Thee, with no blood spilt.
Just bow to me, this one small deed,
And every crown, every land, shall be freed."

LEAH NIFFHONDRO

The offer hung like a bitter curse,
But Jesus saw through the devil's verse.
His eyes aflame, His voice like thunder,
"Get thee hence, O accuser of blunder!
For it is written, worship the Lord alone,
And serve Him only, bow to His throne."
The earth itself seemed to quake and shake,
As the devil fled, with soul at stake.
The winds grew calm, the skies turned clear,
As angels descended, drawing near.
They tended to the Holy One's need,
With gentle care, with love and speed.
For the battle won, though fierce and long,
Had proved the Savior's spirit strong.
The wilderness, where shadows creep,
Had witnessed the devil's final sweep.
But Christ emerged, victorious and true,
With the dawn of hope, born anew.
Each temptation, each whispered lie,
Was met with truth that could not die.
For in the face of darkest night,
Jesus shone with heaven's light.
His hunger deep, His body frail,
Yet His resolve did not fail.
This victory in the desert wild,
Showed the strength of heaven's child.
No bread, no crown, no kingdom's gleam,
Could turn Him from the Father's dream.
For He came to break the chains of sin,
To open the gates and let life in.

So when we face our own dark hour,
Remember Christ, His holy power.
For He has walked the path we tread,
And in His footsteps, we are led.
Through every trial, through every test,
His love sustains, His word is blessed.
In the wilderness, He proved the way,
That in God's word, we find our stay.
The tempter's voice may still resound,
But in Christ's truth, we are found.
For His victory, so fierce, so grand,
Is the rock on which we stand.

The Calling of the Fishermen: A Tide of Destiny

By the shores of Galilee, where the waters sway,
And the morning mist begins to play,
Men of labor, with hands of steel,
Cast their nets with practiced zeal.
Simon and Andrew, James and John,
Toiled through the night, with hope nearly gone.
Their eyes, weary from the sea's embrace,
Yet unaware of their destined place.
The dawn broke soft with a golden hue,
As waves whispered secrets old yet true.
But amidst the calm of the waking tide,
A presence approached, in heaven's stride.
Jesus walked by the water's edge,
His gaze a beacon, a silent pledge.
He saw their hearts, their silent plea,
And knew that they were meant to be free.
"Come, follow me," He called so clear,
"And I will make you fishers of men, draw near."
His voice, like thunder wrapped in grace,
Filled their souls, and time found its place.
They looked at Him, this man unknown,
Yet in His eyes, their futures shone.

The nets they held, once anchors of life,
Now felt like chains in the midst of strife.
Simon's heart, a tempest of doubt,
Felt a calm in the storm, as fear fell out.
For in those words, so simple, so pure,
He found a calling, steadfast and sure.
Andrew, with wonder, felt a fire,
A holy spark, a deep desire.
James and John, the sons of thunder,
Heard the call, their hearts asunder.
They left their boats, their nets behind,
The lives they knew, the paths they'd find.
For in His voice, they felt the flame,
A burning truth, a holy claim.
Their steps, once heavy with the weight of the sea,
Now lightened with hope, with destiny.
The sea that once was their only guide,
Now mirrored the One who walked beside.
No longer bound to the tide's cruel game,
They followed the man who knew their name.
Each step they took, a step in faith,
Each breath they drew, a pledge they made.
The world they knew began to fade,
As a new horizon was softly laid.
In Jesus' eyes, they saw the dawn,
Of a kingdom coming, a world reborn.
Their hearts, now vessels of grace and light,
Set sail with Him, into the night.
For He called them not just from the shore,
But to a life that promised more.

To cast their nets in a deeper sea,
Where souls were lost and sought to be free.
They became the heralds of a love so vast,
A love that would echo, and everlast.
So when they followed, hearts open wide,
They knew the One who walked beside.
For in His call, they found their voice,
A song of purpose, a reason to rejoice.
The fishermen, once bound to earth,
Now carried the message of heaven's birth.
And as they walked that sacred path,
They felt the power of His love's wrath.
Not a wrath of anger or of scorn,
But a fire that cleansed, a soul reborn.
The calling of the first disciples true,
Was a calling that forever grew.
For in their hearts, and in their hands,
They held the future of many lands.
The nets they cast, now filled with grace,
Caught the world in love's embrace.
And in the end, when all is done,
Their journey with Him had just begun.

The First Miracle: Water to Wine, A Sign Divine

In Cana's hills, where the vines do twine,
And the sun kisses the earth with a golden line,
There was a wedding, joyous and grand,
Where love and laughter walked hand in hand.
The guests gathered close, their spirits high,
As music danced beneath the sky.
But in the midst of this joyous cheer,
A quiet worry began to appear.
The wine had run dry, the cups were bare,
And with it, the joy turned to despair.
The whispers spread, the smiles grew thin,
As the hosts feared shame would soon begin.
But Mary, with a mother's grace,
Saw the concern on every face.
She turned to Jesus, her son so dear,
And spoke the words that all would hear.
"They have no wine," she softly said,
And in those words, a prayer was read.
Jesus, with a knowing eye,
Saw the moment, His time was nigh.
But gently He replied with care,
"My hour has not yet come, nor share."

Yet in His heart, He knew the plan,
The first sign of God's love for man.
So He called the servants, willing and true,
And told them what they must do.
"Fill the jars with water," He calmly spoke,
And with those words, the miracle woke.
The jars were filled, to the brim they rose,
With water clear as the mountain's snows.
But as they poured the liquid fine,
It turned, as if by hands divine.
The water blushed, a crimson hue,
As the first drop of wine flowed through.
The steward, surprised, took a sip,
And felt the warmth on his eager lip.
"This is the best," he cried in awe,
"For you've saved the finest I ever saw!"
The guests rejoiced, the feast renewed,
As heaven's gift in wine was brewed.
But in that moment, more than joy,
Was born a truth no time could destroy.
For in that act, so simple and pure,
Jesus revealed a love secure.
He showed that in the common and plain,
The power of God would not abstain.
The water to wine, a sign so bright,
Was more than a wonder, more than a sight.
It was the first glimpse of the grace to come,
When the kingdom of heaven would not be numb.
For just as the water changed its form,
So too would hearts be transformed.

This miracle, in Cana's town,
Began the path that led heaven down.
It whispered of a future day,
When sorrow's night would turn to day.
The wine that flowed, so rich, so sweet,
Was a promise that love would defeat.
For in this sign, the world first saw,
The depth of Christ's redemptive law.
A love that turns the simple into grand,
A grace that lifts with a gentle hand.
And so, the wedding in Cana's light,
Became the dawn of God's delight.
The water to wine, a moment divine,
Marked the start of love's design.
For every drop, both then and now,
Is a symbol of the sacred vow.
That Christ would turn the world's despair,
Into joy beyond compare.

The Healing of Mary: A Miracle of Grace

In the quiet streets where shadows roam,
Where the broken find no home,
A woman walked with a heart so torn,
Her spirit crushed, her hope forlorn.
Mary, her name, with sorrowed eyes,
Carried the weight of countless lies.
Her soul, once bright, now cloaked in pain,
Yearned for light, for freedom's gain.
The whispers followed, the looks of scorn,
As she wandered through the world, so worn.
Her past a burden, too heavy to bear,
Her future a void, filled with despair.
But in the midst of her darkest night,
A rumor spread, a glimmer of light.
Of a man named Jesus, with hands that healed,
A power from heaven, divinely revealed.
With trembling steps, she sought Him out,
Her heart a storm of fear and doubt.
Through the crowd, she pressed her way,
Hoping for a brighter day.
Her faith, though fragile, burned within,
A desperate hope to cleanse her sin.

And there He stood, with eyes so kind,
A love so pure, it filled her mind.
She reached out with a trembling hand,
And touched His robe, unable to stand.
In that instant, her world did change,
The weight she bore began to estrange.
A warmth, a light, filled her soul,
As broken pieces became whole.
Jesus turned, His gaze so clear,
"Who touched Me?" He asked with cheer.
Mary, trembling, fell to her knees,
Her heart released from its agonies.
With tears that flowed like a river's course,
She told her story, with no remorse.
"Daughter," He said, with a voice so sweet,
"Your faith has made you whole, complete.
Go in peace, be free from pain,
For you have found your life again."
His words, a balm to her wounded heart,
Gave her the strength for a fresh start.
The crowd stood still, in awe, in grace,
As they beheld the miracle in her face.
For the woman, once bound by chains,
Was now set free, without remains.
The love of Christ, so vast, so wide,
Had healed the hurt she could not hide.
And Mary, now with joy so pure,
Knew that her healing was secure.
No longer broken, no longer lost,
Her soul was free, at any cost.

For in the touch of the Savior's hand,
She found her place in the promised land.
The miracle of healing, so profound,
Was more than just a body unbound.
It was the start of a life renewed,
A story of grace that was pursued.
For in that moment, Christ revealed,
The power of love, the wounds He healed.
And Mary, now a beacon bright,
Walked in the day, no longer at night.
Her life a testimony, strong and true,
Of what the love of Christ can do.
For in His hands, she found her peace,
And in His words, her soul's release.

DIVINE ECHOES: POEMS OF PROPHETS, FAITH, & REDEMPTION

The Faith of the Centurion: A Soldier's Prayer

In the land where Caesar's banners fly,
And Rome's great eagles pierce the sky,
A soldier stood, with armor worn,
A man of war, by battle torn.
Yet in his heart, a seed was sown,
A whisper of faith, a light unknown.
His servant lay on a bed of pain,
A shadow of life, a hope in vain.
The centurion, with a heart so stern,
Felt the fire of love begin to burn.
He'd heard of a man, a healer, divine,
Who turned water to wine, who healed the blind.
With iron will and soldier's grace,
He sought the healer, face to face.
But as he neared, his steps grew light,
For in his heart, he saw the sight.
A man of power, yet gentle and mild,
Whose voice could calm both storm and child.
He came to Jesus, with head held low,
A warrior's pride, now humbled so.
"Lord," he said, with voice so clear,
"My servant lies in pain severe.

But I am not worthy, this I know,
For you to come where I must go."
"Just say the word, and he'll be healed,
For in Your word, all power is sealed.
I am a man under authority's chain,
I say 'Go,' and they do without disdain.
So if You speak, I know it's done,
For You command as God's own Son."
Jesus turned, with eyes of awe,
At the faith in this man He saw.
"Not in Israel have I found such faith,
As this centurion's humble grace.
Go, your servant's healed, it's true,
By the faith that flows so deep in you."
The centurion bowed, then walked away,
With heart so light, in the light of day.
He found his servant, strong and well,
A miracle told, a tale to tell.
For in that moment, a truth was shown,
That faith alone can move the stone.
No temple's walls, no priestly rite,
Could match the power of faith's pure light.
A soldier's trust, so deep, so vast,
Had broken through the veil at last.
And in that act, so simple, so clear,
The kingdom of heaven drew near.
For it wasn't the rank or the sword he bore,
But the faith that opened heaven's door.
A faith that knew, without a doubt,
That God's own word would cast all out.

LEAH NIFFHONDRO

The centurion's heart, both brave and true,
Was a vessel of light that pierced through.
And so his story, unlike the rest,
Is one of faith that stood the test.
A faith that didn't need to see,
But trusted in the mystery.
The faith of a soldier, strong and bright,
Who found his peace in heaven's light.

The Fall of the Forerunner: The Beheading of John the Baptist

In Herod's court, where shadows creep,
And power's hand does secrets keep,
A prophet's voice, so bold, so clear,
Echoed truths that kings would fear.
John, the Baptist, clothed in grace,
With fire in his eyes, and truth on his face,
He spoke of sin, of wrongs made right,
A beacon in the darkest night.
But in the halls where pride did reign,
His words were met with cold disdain.
Herodias, with a vengeful heart,
Plotted to tear his life apart.
For John had dared to call her sin,
To name the darkness she lived within.
Herod, torn by fear and pride,
Knew John spoke truth, yet couldn't abide.
For though he marveled at the prophet's might,
He feared the power of his sight.
And so, in a dungeon, cold and bare,
John awaited, in silent prayer.
Then came the night of Herod's feast,
Where wine and revelry never ceased.

LEAH NIFFHONDRO

Herodias' daughter, with beauty rare,
Danced before them, with a beguiling stare.
Her movements, like a serpent's glide,
Caught Herod's eye, ignited his pride.
In his drunken joy, he made a vow,
"Ask what you will, and I'll allow.
Even half my kingdom shall be yours,
Just name your wish, and it's yours."
The girl, with a heart untouched by fear,
Whispered her wish in Herod's ear.
Guided by her mother's hate,
She asked for John's most dire fate.
"Give me his head, on a silver plate,
The head of John, to seal his fate."
Herod froze, his blood ran cold,
For in this request, his doom was told.
Yet bound by his word, his foolish pride,
He could not turn the request aside.
The order was given, the deed was done,
As darkness fell, the moonless sun.
In the cell where John did pray,
The guards approached, with swords at play.
He bowed his head, with no remorse,
For he knew this was God's own course.
With one swift stroke, the blade did fall,
And John's voice was silenced in that hall.
But as his head was placed on a tray,
His spirit soared, his soul did sway.
For though his body was laid to rest,
His voice lived on, his truth professed.

DIVINE ECHOES: POEMS OF PROPHETS, FAITH, & REDEMPTION

The kingdom mourned, the heavens wept,
As John, the Baptist, in peace slept.
The prophets cried, the angels sang,
As heaven's gates with glory rang.
For in his death, a seed was sown,
A path of light, to God's own throne.
His blood, like a river, flowed so free,
A testament to what would be.
Herod's court, where shadows dwell,
Could not silence the truth he'd tell.
For John, the herald, paved the way,
For the coming dawn, the brightest day.
His death, though cruel, was not in vain,
For through his loss, the world would gain.
The Lamb would come, the cross would rise,
And in that act, death would despise.
For John, the Baptist, though he fell,
Would see his Savior break the spell.
His voice, once silenced, would rise again,
In every heart, in every amen.
So we remember, with tears and pain,
The prophet's loss, the martyr's gain.
For in his death, the truth was sealed,
A love so strong, it cannot yield.
John, the Baptist, bold and true,
Your voice lives on, in me, in you.

The Rock's Revelation: Peter's Wild Confession

In the shadows of Caesarea's ancient stone,
Where whispers of gods and kings had grown,
The Twelve walked close, with hearts unsure,
As the world around them sought a cure.
But in the midst of the world's vast noise,
A question rose from the One whose voice,
Could calm the storm and heal the blind—
A question that would shake mankind.
"Who do men say that I am?" He asked,
His eyes like fire, His voice unmasked.
The disciples spoke of what they'd heard,
Of prophets and legends, each in turn.
But then He paused, with gaze so deep,
A silence that made their spirits leap.
"And who do you say I am?" He pressed,
A challenge laid upon their chests.
The world seemed to stop, the air grew thin,
As each man searched the depths within.
But it was Peter, bold and wild,
Who broke the silence, heaven's child.
With eyes alight and voice unchained,
He declared the truth, his soul unstained.

"You are the Christ, the Son of the Living God!"
The words burst forth like a lightning rod.
The earth itself seemed to tremble and sway,
As Peter's confession lit the way.
In that moment, time unraveled,
The mystery of ages was now unraveled.
Jesus smiled, a fire in His eyes,
For He knew the truth beneath the skies.
"Blessed are you, Simon, son of Jonah,"
He spoke with a voice like a mighty corona.
"For flesh and blood have not revealed this to you,
But My Father in heaven, who is ever true."
"I tell you this," He said with power,
"On this rock, in this very hour,
I will build My church, and the gates of hell,
Shall not prevail, nor sound their knell.
What you bind on earth shall be bound above,
What you loose below, loosed in love."
Peter's heart raced, his mind aflame,
As the weight of his words became his name.
The Rock, the cornerstone, the base,
Of a kingdom forged by heaven's grace.
Yet in his soul, a tempest brewed,
For he knew not all that he'd pursued.
This was not just a simple claim,
But a call to bear the world's great flame.
To carry the cross, to face the night,
To stand in the face of death's cold might.
For Peter knew, with wild delight,
That his confession was a blazing light.

The winds howled wild, the heavens roared,
As Peter's soul in faith soared.
He had glimpsed the truth, the holy fire,
The Son of God, his heart's desire.
But in that truth, a shadow fell,
Of trials to come, of battles that swell.
For the Christ he named, the God he knew,
Would soon walk a path few pursue.
A path of pain, of thorns and blood,
A sacrifice beyond the flood.
But Peter, wild, with spirit untamed,
Held to the truth he boldly claimed.
In that confession, fierce and bright,
Was born the church, the dawn of light.
A wild, insane, and holy cry,
That echoed through the earth and sky.
Peter's words, like thunder, rolled,
And in their wake, a story told.
Of a faith that leaps into the flame,
Of a love that bears the sacred name.
Peter's confession, a wild embrace,
Of the Son of God, of boundless grace.
And in that moment, fierce and grand,
The Rock was forged by heaven's hand.

The Anointing at Bethany: A Fragrance of Love and Tears

In Bethany's quiet, where shadows fall,
In a house where voices softly call,
A feast was spread, the candles low,
And in the midst, a light did glow.
Jesus sat with eyes serene,
His path ahead both clear and keen.
But in that room, where peace held sway,
A woman came, with no words to say.
Her heart was wild, her spirit torn,
By love so deep, by pain reborn.
She carried with her an alabaster jar,
A treasure of nard, worth more by far,
Than gold or silver, than pearls or spice,
Yet in her hands, it held no price.
For in that jar, she placed her all,
In a single act, she'd rise or fall.
Without a word, she knelt down low,
Her tears began to freely flow.
She broke the jar, its seal undone,
And poured the oil, her only one.
The fragrance filled the room with grace,
As she anointed the Master's face.

It flowed like rivers, pure and sweet,
A sacrifice laid at His feet.
The disciples watched, their eyes wide,
But Judas spoke, with words that chide.
"Why this waste?" he cried in disdain,
"This could have fed the poor, the lame!"
But Jesus, with a gentle glance,
Saw beyond the circumstance.
"Leave her be," He softly said,
"For she has done this for My head."
Her tears mingled with the oil's glow,
As she wept for the love she'd never show.
For she knew the path He'd soon embrace,
The cross, the nails, the world's disgrace.
But in this moment, she gave her best,
A gift of love, of peace, of rest.
"This is for My burial," He spoke with care,
A prophecy hidden in the fragrant air.
The room grew still, the world outside,
As heaven and earth seemed to collide.
Her act of love, so wild, so bold,
Would be remembered, as He foretold.
The oil dripped down, a holy stream,
A liquid prayer, a broken dream.
And as she wiped His feet with hair,
Her soul laid bare, her deepest prayer.
The fragrance lingered, sweet and strong,
A melody without a song.
For in that moment, time stood still,
As love poured out by sheer will.

She anointed the King, not with a crown,
But with the tears of a love unbound.
A love that knew no bounds, no end,
A love that would soon descend,
To the darkest depths, to death's own door,
To rise again, forevermore.
Her sacrifice, her broken heart,
Was a masterpiece, a work of art.
For in that jar, in that single act,
Was the gospel's truth, the purest fact.
That love is wild, and love is free,
And in that love, we all must be.
The room was filled with heaven's scent,
A testament to love's intent.
For she anointed not just a man,
But the Lamb of God, the Great I Am.
And in that room, where shadows fall,
Love broke the jar and gave its all.
So when we speak of Bethany's day,
Remember the love that paved the way.
The crazy, wild, and reckless grace,
That poured from her heart in that holy place.
For in her tears, in her fragrant plea,
We find the depth of love's decree.

The Trial and the Denial: A Night of Shadows and Tears

In the cold, dark halls of Pilate's court,
Where justice was twisted and mercy was short,
The Son of Man stood silent and still,
As the world conspired to break His will.
The crowds, like wolves, with hate in their eyes,
Shouted for blood, demanding their prize.
The weight of the world on His shoulders pressed,
As lies were spoken, and truth suppressed.
His hands were bound, His heart laid bare,
Before the ones who did not care.
Soldiers mocked with a crown of thorn,
As heaven wept for a world forlorn.
Pilate's voice, uncertain and weak,
Asked the crowd what fate to seek.
"Crucify Him!" they screamed with might,
And darkness fell on that dreadful night.
But outside the court, in the courtyard dim,
Peter stood with fear in him.
The one who swore to never depart,
Now felt the terror grip his heart.
Three times the question came his way,
"Weren't you with Him, tell us, say?"

And three times Peter, with trembling breath,
Denied his Lord, sealing his own death.
"I do not know Him!" he cried in fear,
As his soul was torn, as his heart did sear.
The cock crowed loud in the breaking dawn,
And Peter's face grew pale and drawn.
He remembered then the words foretold,
How his faith would falter, how his love would fold.
Tears streamed down his rugged face,
As he fled the scene, consumed by disgrace.
Inside, the trial continued on,
With every hope and mercy gone.
Jesus, silent, bore the scorn,
His body bruised, His spirit worn.
He saw the faces, twisted, cruel,
The hearts of stone, the minds of fools.
Yet in His eyes, no anger burned,
Just a love that would not be turned.
He knew the cost, He knew the price,
To save the lost, the ultimate sacrifice.
The weight of sin, the world's great wrong,
He bore it all, so firm, so strong.
And as they led Him to the cross,
Where love and pain would soon emboss,
The heavens trembled, the earth did quake,
For all creation was at stake.
Peter, in the shadows, wept,
His soul in anguish, no peace, no rest.
How could he, who loved so deep,
Fall so far, so low, so steep?

LEAH NIFFHONDRO

His heart was shattered, his spirit torn,
As he mourned the night when he'd been reborn,
Not in faith, but in a flood of tears,
As he faced his darkest fears.
Jesus, on trial, betrayed by His own,
Stood as the cornerstone of a love unknown.
Peter, in the courtyard, lost and alone,
Felt the crushing weight of what he had sown.
But even in that hour, so dark, so dire,
A spark of hope, a tiny fire,
Glimmered faint in the depths of despair,
For the love of Christ was everywhere.
The trial would end, the cross would rise,
And Peter's tears would cleanse his eyes.
For in his failure, in his shame,
He found the mercy in Jesus' name.
A night of shadows, a night of dread,
But through it all, a path was tread,
That led to life, that led to grace,
Where every tear has its place.
And though Peter wept, and Jesus bled,
The story was far from being dead.
For in that trial, in that denial,
Was the seed of faith, of hope's revival.
A shocking truth, a love so deep,
That even in betrayal's steep,
God's plan was moving, firm and bright,
Turning the darkest night to light.

The Crucifixion: The World's Darkest Hour

On a hill called Golgotha, where shadows cling,
Where the earth itself began to sing
A dirge of sorrow, of pain and loss,
The Son of God hung on a cross.
Nails driven deep through flesh and bone,
A crown of thorns, His only throne.
His body broken, His blood poured out,
As the heavens wept, and angels shouted.
The sky grew dark, the sun refused to shine,
As creation mourned this cruel design.
The crowds below, with hearts of stone,
Mocked the One who bore their own.
"King of the Jews!" they spat in scorn,
Unknowing that for them He was born.
With every lash, with every tear,
The weight of the world was drawing near.
His mother stood, with eyes of grief,
Her heart torn apart, beyond belief.
She watched her Son, her precious Child,
Now despised, rejected, and reviled.
Her tears fell like a river's flow,
As the sword of sorrow struck her low.

Beside her, John, the beloved one,
Felt the pain of what must be done.
"Father, forgive them," He cried aloud,
As the cross stood firm, tall, and proud.
"Forgive them, for they know not what they do,"
A plea of mercy, pure and true.
But in His voice, the agony,
Of bearing sin for all humanity.
Every lie, every sin, every shame,
He carried it all, He bore our blame.
The earth trembled, the rocks were split,
As the Lamb of God endured each hit.
His breath grew shallow, His strength did fade,
As the price of love was fully paid.
"My God, My God, why hast Thou forsaken?"
In that moment, the world was shaken.
For the Son of Man, in His darkest hour,
Felt the sting of death's full power.
But even then, amidst the pain,
He saw the joy, the future gain.
"It is finished," He whispered, soft and clear,
As His spirit left, and death drew near.
The veil was torn, the temple shook,
As the gates of heaven He undertook.
The earth held its breath, the silence screamed,
As the hope of the world hung, it seemed.
The soldiers stood in stunned dismay,
As the Son of God had passed away.
A centurion, with eyes of awe,
Proclaimed the truth he saw.

"Truly, this was the Son of God,"
As tears fell on the blood-stained sod.
The world had never known such loss,
As the day the Savior took the cross.
But in that death, so dark, so deep,
Was planted a seed that would not sleep.
For in three days, the stone would roll,
And from the grave would rise His soul.
The cross, a symbol of death and pain,
Became the sign of love's great gain.
For in His sacrifice, in His final breath,
He conquered sin, He conquered death.
So let the world remember this,
The agony, the final kiss,
Of love so pure, of grace so wide,
That it could not be denied.
The crucifixion, a moment in time,
Where the world's sin met the divine.
And though the tears still freely flow,
They are the tears that make us grow.
For in His pain, we find our peace,
In His death, our souls' release.
The cross of Christ, the world's great cost,
Was the moment when all was not lost.
So let us weep, let us mourn,
But know that in His death, we are reborn.
The crucifixion, the darkest night,
Is the dawn of eternal light.

LEAH NIFFHONDRO

The Burial and Resurrection: A Triumph Over Death

In the stillness of a Friday's grief,
Where sorrow wrapped the world in disbelief,
They took His body, broken, cold,
The Lamb of God, so brave, so bold.
His lifeless form, once full of grace,
Now bore the marks of death's embrace.
The cross, now empty, cast its shade,
As His followers wept, their hopes decayed.
Joseph of Arimathea, with tender care,
Carried Him from the cross, with heart laid bare.
In linen pure, they wrapped Him tight,
Preparing Him for the tomb's cold night.
The stone, so heavy, rolled in place,
Sealing the tomb, an empty space.
The world seemed lost, the light grown dim,
As death held fast to the body of Him.
The sun set low, the earth stood still,
As the shadows deepened on Calvary's hill.
The world in mourning, hearts in pain,
As they wondered if they'd see Him again.
The women wept, their tears like rain,
As hope seemed drowned in a sea of pain.

The tomb, so silent, the night so long,
Yet in that silence, a hidden song.
For in the depths of that cold, dark tomb,
Where death had laid its final doom,
A spark of life began to stir,
A light within, a holy blur.
The earth trembled, the stone did quake,
As heaven's power began to break.
The chains of death, so strong, so tight,
Could not hold back the Lord of Light.
On the third day, as dawn's first breath,
Began to chase away the night of death,
The stone was rolled, the grave was bare,
For life had triumphed over despair.
Jesus, risen, with wounds so bright,
Stepped forth into the morning light.
His body, glorified and new,
Was proof that every word was true.
The women came, with spices sweet,
To anoint the body, to bow at His feet.
But they found the stone rolled away,
And the tomb where He lay was empty that day.
Their hearts raced with fear and wonder,
As an angel's voice split the air asunder:
"Why seek the living among the dead?
He is not here, He has risen," he said.
Tears of joy replaced their dread,
As they recalled the words He'd said.
The promise that death would not prevail,
That love would rise, would never fail.

They ran to tell the others the news,
But disbelief clouded their views.
Yet Peter, bold, ran to see,
And found the truth, the victory.
Jesus, alive, appeared to them all,
Breaking the curse, reversing the fall.
His hands, His feet, still bore the scars,
But in His eyes shone the morning stars.
He breathed on them, His peace bestowed,
As the seeds of faith within them sowed.
"Go forth," He said, "and tell the world,
That death is conquered, love unfurled."
The burial, once a sign of loss,
Now marked the turning of the cross.
The resurrection, bright and clear,
Declared that God was always near.
The grave could not hold the Son of Man,
For His was a higher, divine plan.
To break the chains of sin and death,
And give to all eternal breath.
The world was shocked, the heavens sang,
As the bells of victory loudly rang.
The resurrection, a blaze of light,
Turned the darkest night into the brightest sight.
No tomb, no stone, no power on earth,
Could hold back the Lord of endless worth.
For in His rise, we all are free,
From the bonds of death, eternally.
So let the world be filled with praise,
For the One who rose on the third day.

His death, His burial, a passing phase,
For in His life, we find our way.
The resurrection, a story bold,
Of love that never grows old.
A tale of power, grace, and might,
That turned the grave into a source of light.
Let tears flow, let hearts be stirred,
For the greatest story ever heard.
The burial and resurrection of Christ,
The ultimate sacrifice, the ultimate price.
He lives, He reigns, forevermore,
And in His name, our spirits soar.
The tomb is empty, the grave undone,
For Jesus, our Savior, has truly won.

The Road to Emmaus: Hearts Ablaze in the Night

In the fading light of a sorrowful day,
Two walked the road to Emmaus, away,
From the shattered dreams and hopes undone,
Their hearts heavy with what had begun.
Cleopas and his friend, with faces drawn,
Spoke of the crucifixion, the darkness of dawn.
Their faith, once strong, now faint and weak,
As they struggled to find the words to speak.
But as they walked, in the twilight's hue,
A stranger joined, unnoticed at first view.
His steps were light, His presence calm,
A soothing voice, a healing balm.
"What is it," He asked, "that weighs you so?
Why do you walk with heads hung low?"
They turned to Him, with eyes of pain,
And shared their grief, their endless strain.
"Have You not heard?" they asked, surprised,
Of the One they called Jesus, the One who died?
A prophet mighty in word and deed,
Who healed the sick, who met every need.
But our leaders condemned Him to the cross,
And now we're lost in a sea of loss.

We had hoped He would redeem us all,
But now we stand with hearts so small."
The stranger listened, His heart aligned,
With every sorrow, every tear confined.
Then He began to speak of old,
The prophecies and stories told.
"Was it not written," He softly said,
"That the Christ must suffer, then rise from the dead?"
He spoke of Moses, the Psalms, the Law,
Unfolding mysteries that left them in awe.
Their hearts burned within, their spirits soared,
As the scriptures opened, as truth was poured.
Yet still, they knew not the Stranger's name,
Until they reached their destination, just the same.
"Stay with us," they urged with plea,
"For the night is near, and we long to see."
He agreed and sat with them to dine,
And in that moment, the world aligned.
He took the bread, and blessed it so,
Then broke it, and their eyes did glow.
For in that simple, sacred act,
They saw the truth, the hidden fact.
It was Jesus, the Lord, alive, revealed,
The wounds of love, forever healed.
But as they gazed in wonder's might,
He vanished from their astonished sight.
With hearts aflame, they could not stay,
They raced back to Jerusalem without delay.
To tell the others what they had seen,
The risen Lord, no longer a dream.

The night was deep, but their spirits soared,
As they proclaimed the glory of the Lord.

Jesus Appears to the Disciples: Peace in the Storm

In the upper room, where fear held sway,
The disciples gathered, with no words to say.
The door was locked, the world outside,
Seemed filled with danger, nowhere to hide.
But suddenly, in the midst of their fright,
Jesus appeared, a beacon of light.
"Peace be with you," He gently spoke,
And the chains of fear began to break.
Their hearts, once bound by doubt and dread,
Now leaped with joy as He stood ahead.
His hands, His side, the wounds He bore,
A testimony to love's great war.
Thomas, the doubter, with eyes wide,
Reached out to touch the pierced side.
"Be not faithless, but believe,"
And in that touch, he did perceive.
"My Lord and my God!" he cried aloud,
As tears of joy fell in a shroud.
For in that moment, doubt was slain,
And faith was born in love's sweet pain.
Jesus smiled, with a voice so clear,
"Blessed are those who believe without fear."

The room was filled with heaven's song,
As the disciples knew where they belonged.

The Reinstatement of Peter: A Love Unbroken

By the Sea of Galilee, in the morning mist,
Peter stood, with a heart full of twists.
The memories of denial, of tears and shame,
Burned in his soul like a relentless flame.
He had vowed to follow, to never depart,
Yet thrice he denied, with a trembling heart.
But as the dawn broke with a golden ray,
He saw Jesus standing, calling his way.
"Come, have breakfast," the Savior called,
And in those words, Peter's heart was enthralled.
They sat by the fire, with fish and bread,
Yet Peter's soul was filled with dread.
Would the Lord remember, would He condemn?
Or could he be restored once again?
Jesus turned, with eyes so kind,
And asked the question that weighed on his mind.
"Simon, son of John, do you love Me more than these?"
Peter's heart sank, brought to his knees.
"Yes, Lord, You know that I love You true."
"Then feed My lambs," was the call to pursue.
Again the question, piercing and deep,
"Do you love Me?" it made Peter weep.

"Yes, Lord, You know that I love You," he cried,
"Then tend My sheep," was the Lord's reply.
A third time the question, a mirror of pain,
"Do you love Me?" the words were plain.
Peter, grieved, with tears that fell,
Said, "Lord, You know all, You know me well.
You know that I love You, with all I am."
"Then feed My sheep," was the divine command.
The air was thick with love's embrace,
As Peter saw the Savior's face.
No condemnation, no trace of scorn,
But a love that had been there since he was born.
"Follow Me," Jesus softly said,
And Peter knew, the past was dead.
The road to Emmaus, the upper room,
The Sea of Galilee, where flowers bloom—
All these moments, stitched in time,
Wove a story, so pure, so divine.
The risen Christ, with hands so scarred,
Reached into hearts, once broken, marred.
He turned their sorrow into song,
Their fears to faith, so deep, so strong.
And Peter, once lost, was found anew,
In the love of the One who made all things true.
For in that dawn, by Galilee's shore,
He was restored, to fall no more.
And so the world, in shock and awe,
Beholds the story that changes law.
For in His death, and in His rise,
The truth of love never dies.

LEAH NIFFHONDRO

The road to Emmaus, the touch of peace,
The reinstatement of love's release—
These are the tales that shape our days,
And guide us in life's winding ways.
For Jesus lives, and love prevails,
Through every doubt, through all travails.
And in His wounds, we find our home,
No longer lost, no more to roam.
The world may tremble, kingdoms fall,
But the love of Christ surpasses all.

The Ascension: Heaven's Open Door

On the Mount of Olives, where the breeze did sigh,
Underneath the vast and endless sky,
The disciples stood with hearts in awe,
Witnesses to the final law.
The risen Christ, with wounds still shown,
Gathered His own, His voice a tone,
Of love and peace, of hope renewed,
A promise kept, a truth pursued.
His eyes, like fire, with grace imbued,
Looked upon them, as He stood.
"No longer shall you be alone,
For the Spirit comes, as I have shown.
Go into the world, in every land,
And preach the gospel, My command.
Baptize the nations, teach them all,
To follow the way, to heed the call."
Their hearts were torn, both joy and pain,
For they knew He would depart again.
But in His words, a comfort lay,
That through His absence, they'd find their way.
He blessed them there, with hands upraised,
And in that moment, all were amazed.
Then slowly, gently, He began to rise,

Lifting His body towards the skies.
The earth beneath felt a holy quake,
As heaven reached down, the bond to break.
The clouds, like chariots, swift and bright,
Carried Him upwards, out of sight.
Yet in that upward, glorious flight,
He left a trail of eternal light.
The disciples watched with tear-filled eyes,
As their Lord ascended to the skies.
Their hearts, now full of wonder's might,
Grasped the mystery of the night.
For though He left, He wasn't gone,
His presence lingered, like the dawn.
A promise made, a promise kept,
In their souls, His words still crept.
"Why do you stand, looking to the sky?"
An angel's voice from on high,
Broke the silence, pierced the air,
As the disciples felt despair.
"This Jesus, whom you've seen ascend,
Will return to you, this is not the end."
With these words, their hearts were stirred,
And in their spirits, courage spurred.
They knew their task, their mission clear,
To spread His love, to cast out fear.
For in His ascension, heaven's gate,
Opened wide, to seal their fate.
No longer bound by earthly ties,
Their mission lay beyond the skies.
And so they went, with hearts ablaze,

To carry His name through all their days.
Yet in their minds, that vision stayed,
Of Jesus, lifted, unafraid.
His hands still raised, His face so bright,
A beacon in the darkest night.
The world was changed, the heavens wide,
For Christ ascended, glorified.
And though the tears did freely flow,
They knew the truth, they'd come to know.
That in His leaving, they were found,
For in His absence, love unbound.
The sky itself seemed to weep that day,
As the Son of Man was borne away.
But in those tears, a promise lay,
That He would return, in glory's ray.
And until that day, they'd hold the light,
Of His ascension, pure and bright.
For Jesus, now at heaven's throne,
Would guide them still, though not alone.
The Spirit, sent in tongues of fire,
Would fill their hearts with holy desire.
To preach, to heal, to make Him known,
Until the day He calls them home.
So let the world, in awe, recall,
The day when Christ rose above all.
The Ascension, a moment so divine,
When heaven and earth did intertwine.
And in that sky, so blue, so wide,
The path to glory opened wide.
The disciples left that sacred place,

With a fire that nothing could erase.
For they had seen the Lord ascend,
And knew His love would never end.
The Ascension, a tale of might,
A story of love, a guiding light.
And in the hearts of those who believe,
The truth of that day will never leave.
For Jesus, risen, now reigns on high,
Yet with us still, He draws nigh.
In every prayer, in every breath,
We feel the power of His death.
And in His rising, in His flight,
We find our hope, our endless light.

www.ingramcontent.com/pod-product-compliance
Lightning Source LLC
Chambersburg PA
CBHW020454180726
47992CB00027B/2227